SALT OF THE EARTH

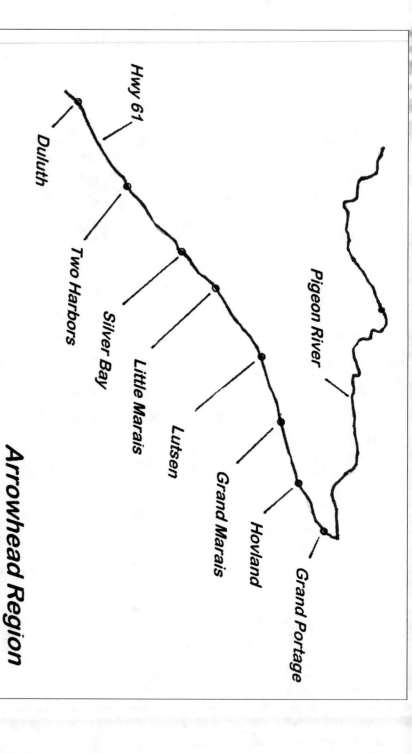

Arrowhead Region
Of Minnesota

Map is the sole work of the author

Hwy 61

Duluth

Two Harbors

Silver Bay

Little Marais

Lutsen

Grand Marais

Hovland

Grand Portage

Pigeon River

SALT OF THE EARTH

A History of Hovland, Minnesota, and Its People

David P. Holmes

North Star Press of St. Cloud, Inc.

St.Cloud, Minnesota

First Edition, June 2010

Printed in the United States of America

Published by
North Star Press of St. Cloud, Inc.
P.O. Box 451
St. Cloud, Minnesota 56302

www.northstarpress.com

Chapter 1

The small town of Hovland, Minnesota, sits unobtrusively on Minnesota Highway 61 as it stretches from Duluth and Grand Marais to the Canadian border. Nestled on the shore of mighty Lake Superior, the town sits as a muted reminder that it is there because people put it there. Traveling halfway around the globe in primitive conveyances, homes and established lives were left behind to seek freedom, fame, fortune, or just adventure. Children were born, people died, the weak moved, and the strong stayed. As their homes were erected and the fields were plowed and the traps set, their town grew around them.

The remnants of the stalwart are still in place today, living by the same values and determination their ancestors instilled in them. Bloodlines reaching back to the first foot being placed on the shore, and of the people that were close behind, still pump through the hearts and souls of the few remaining families that call Hovland home.

This book is not a family chronicle. The stories that have been put onto these pages came from the collections of many people who were perceptive enough to love and respect the families that preceded them. Tales passed on, events recorded in bibles and journals, clippings, and photographs, have been assembled to tell the history that helped

Hovland become a town. The most concise information came from the incredible memory of Virginia Johnson. Her daughter, Dusty Nelms (Johnson) has spent years putting data collected from her mother, and primarily her aunt Millie Mainella who has turned 100 years recently, into a file just to preserve it. History forgotten is history lost, and Dusty was not going to let that happen.

The Johnson's, Sundquist's, Bergsven's, and Schuppel's, weren't the first and weren't the only families to step onto the Lake Superior shoreline in Chicago Bay. But, they are still there today, working and trying just as hard as ever to raise their children and leave a legacy they will be proud of.

Thanks and appreciation is extended to all contributors who trusted me with the valuable family heirlooms that go into the recording of the history of Hovland Minnesota.

Millie Johnson Mainella.

Chapter 2

E ARLY LIFE IN THE ARROWHEAD region of Minnesota was hard, but the trappers worked the streams and forests in spite of the severity of weather and terrain that confronted them. They were a hardy and determined group that bent into the work and did what needed to be done. In the late 1600s, French explorers led an expedition into the Minnesota territory, followed by fur traders for French and British companies. The fruits of their labor were the prized beaver pelts that would eventually decorate the heads of stylish Europeans and Eastern Americans. Later, as the fur adornment trend waned, timber would be the gold that maintained penetration into the cold north.

First inhabited by Dakota and Ojibwa, also known as Chippewa or Anishinabe, the white man pushed the Native Americans further west. Some stayed, trying to integrate with the white man as he ravaged the land. Others moved on to find their fate in places like Little Big Horn and Wounded Knee.

Had the federal promise of money to buy food and supplies been implemented the way it was intended, the history of the region would have been vastly different. A majority of Native Americans showed a willingness to live in harmony with the whites, but prejudice and government intervention changed everything.

Rich in the resources that turned dreamers into adventurers, the allure of freedom, and the most prized possession of all, land, hopeful wanderers settle in the lush, pristine paradise of the Minnesota Arrowhead.

The influx of settlers from Finland, Norway, Germany, and Sweden brought a robust people willing to carve their future out of dense forests and unforgiving winters. If they didn't die from the cold and lived through the heat and insect infestations of summer, they were likely to live another year, watching their families grow and blend into the towns and villages growing around them.

We look with awe and deep respect at what these people did, but to them it was what they *had* to do if they were to survive. Some of the families that started a new life in the Arrowhead were forced to move on, some perished, and some are still living there among the memories and footholds their ancestors left for them.

The few remaining families with roots so deep that the community was built around them survive today because they had the courage, faith, and strength to hang on. This story is a compilation of family history and recollections of the pioneers who settled on the North Shore of Lake Superior, in Minnesota, to form what has become the tiny nondescript town of Hovland.

There are still families who live in Hovland today that have deep roots and connections to the settlers who first came ashore in Chicago Bay. This story emanates from the records of one of those families and other contributors. Still unpretentious and hard working, these people have survived the rigors of life in a harsh, yet beautiful, paradise because there was no other choice. This is home, and this is where they belong.

My APPRECIATION IS EXTENDED to the Duane and Virginia Johnson family of Hovland, Minnesota, for their support. The reason I chose this particular family was the bond that was handed down from one generation to the next. The diligence and ethics that pushed the ancestors is the same quality that I see in them today.

This story started long before I came along. I just found the fascination that compelled me to write about it. Dusty (Johnson) Nelms was one of many contributors who had spent years collecting her family history, and with the amazing memory of her mother, to add to it. With the blessings of the Johnson family, I proudly present the story of "Modern pioneers, who are still . . . *the salt of the earth.*"

Saturday, June 26, 2008
Hovland, Minnesota

THIS IS HOW IT STARTED and how I became involved.

Through the friendship of their parents, my wife and I had known Kathi and Rusty Johnson for over twenty years. When we received an invitation to the ceremony to renew their wedding vows, we were delighted. Appropriately, the ceremony was to take place on their twenty-fifth wedding anniversary.

We have been friends of Kathi's parents, Bob and Jeanine Swearingen, for a period of time that seems to stretch indefinitely. Along with Bob's lifelong friends, Curt and Marge Mueller, these were people we knew and loved, spending innumerable weekends laughing and telling jokes and often playing silly tricks on each other.

The day before the celebration, we packed up the fifth wheel camper, dragged it up north to Hovland, and parked in Bob's yard. This is not just a yard. Standing and facing west, one gazes over a low valley that rises into a high ridge miles away. Covered with a light mist settling into the tops of thousands of luscious pines, the sight is breathtaking. It is a view that begs for a belief in God.

If Bob could add two-hundred pounds, three-feet of height, plus grow a bushy beard, he would be Grizzly Adams. At home in the environs of the woods, it is his lifelong dream.

On our arrival, Bob told us, "A wolf has been hanging around, so be careful at night." Of course, there is always the thought that a bear may be rumbling through the woods, also.

As expected, a fresh pot of coffee was waiting, and we are all looking forward to a long weekend laughing at silly jokes, playing the dice game 10,000, and arguing over even sillier politics.

That night, at a campfire in Bob's yard up by the pond, at least several dozen arms belonging to members of the wedding party extending hot dogs over the flames. Someone brought a pan of chocolate bars, and anyone with an empty hand would likely get a can of beer stuck in it by one of Bob's exuberant sons, Shawn and Paul.

That's the way of life with our friends. If someone notices that you have a need, they fill it. And people in this part of the country often trade for goods or services. If a man has a backhoe, he might dig a septic pit in exchange for truck repair, or a side of venison. Barter is common here.

Laughter and the reminiscing of wondrous past times fostered a warm comfortable feeling of friendship around the fire. Of course Rusty, the groom (again) took the brunt of our teasing about his second honeymoon, but he took it well. With a smile, no less, so the jibes were obviously well placed.

Rusty Johnson is one of those people who just seem to make life happen, not only for himself, but for his family and friends as well. When he married Kathi Swearingen on June 25, 1983, the two worked together to build their house by setting up his dad's sawmill on the property and creating lumber out of timber. The heating system, flooring, siding, and all the rest came by way of hard work.

Kathi's mother, Jeanine Swearingen, has family roots extending up to the Rydens at the border, being related to Aunt Mable and Ed Ryden, who was known affectionately as "Big Ed." Aunt Mable and Ed were the original Rydens to own the Border Store. Located at the end of old Highway 61, nothing remains today except a few crumbling foundations and the abutments for the bridge that used to cross the Pigeon River. Today, the existing Border Store is a thriving business located at the entrance to Canada on the new Highway 61. A nice restaurant, souvenirs, gifts, and the duty-free shop greet Canadian arrivals and the last stop for travelers from the American side.

Jeanine's cousin, Joy Carlson, Mabel and Ed's daughter, lives just up Highway 61 from Hovland with her husband, Joe. Joe Carlson himself is a fascinating story. I love to listen to Joe's adventures of commercial fishing off the coast of Alaska.

At one time, Kathi's parents ran a campground located on the Pigeon River, the dividing line between the United States and Canada. Here they raised their offspring—Kathi, Paul, and Shawn. The early life of the Swearingen children, raised in this pristine chapel of natural beauty, is the embodiment that can be seen in them today. Bob took special pride in showing the huge rock that stood up in the river, battling the current rushing to the 120-foot, High Falls. Standing in the proper position, one could faintly see the carvings in the face of it that a trapper had etched so many years ago. There are still remnants of the ancient nine mile portage created by the Indians, stretching from Lake Superior to bypass the falls.

In 1989, a joint effort by Minnesota and the Grand Portage Band of Chippewa turned the site into the Grand Portage State Park. While creating a beautiful setting for tourists to enjoy, the traces of early history that were so personal to Bob and his family now can be enjoyed by the public. The rock, an eratic deposited by glaciers an eon ago, remains in the river, but the etchings on its surface attest to a far more recent human history of an industry that has passed.

Kathi is definitely a prize, so all it took was for Rusty to convince her parents he was acceptable material for her husband. The decisive factor came when Rusty called on Kathi for a date, to be met at the door by Jeanine's brother, Uncle Darwin Potvin. Knowing Uncle Darwin was to love him for what he was; a good friend. A huge overwhelming bulk of a man, he held a twinkle in his eye that was always warm; and mischievous. However, that particular evening, six-foot-three-inch Uncle Darwin, weighing in at well over two-hundred pounds, met Rusty at the door. His immense girth all but shaded the door opening, cradling a twelve-gauge shotgun in his arms. Rusty gasped, hiding the, "Oh, my God," under his breath. I recall sitting by the campfire at Uncle Darwin's Memorial Day get-together in Brainerd, listening to Darwin retell the story and watching the red climb up Rusty's face. With his typical grin, he took the teasing well.

Rusty Johnson is an amazingly creative man. On one occasion, he needed an extra bench for visitors, so out came the chainsaw, and to the amazement of onlookers, he transformed a log into an eight-foot bench. From building their home to creating the pond in front of the house, whatever Rusty set out to do, he did with skill. He built a pole building to give him a place to repaire autos. The day before the re-enactment of their vows, a friend trashed the transmission in his truck pulling a boat out of the water. Rusty was the obvious man to see.

When Bob's son Shawn got married, the starter in Bob's Mercury went out. On the day of the wedding, Rusty found the right replacement, laid on his back in the parking lot of the church, and replaced it.

Of course Rusty has his "all too human" side, and I suppose he will spend a long time trying to squelch conversations concerning the skunk in the town hall. In all fairness to Kathi, we won't mention who left the door to the town hall open when she went to clean it.

Rusty Johnson is embedded with the talent and skills needed to survive and raise a family in this environment. In spite of twenty-first century technology, it is still a daily struggle to maintain an income and meet obligations. Dwarfed by the same forests that their ancestors faced, the struggle, while more comfortable, is still there.

To most people, there is no amazement to Rusty's talents; it's just what he does.

My respect and admiration for the man has never faltered. As we watch his three boys grow into manhood, we can readily see those same values in them. Still in their teens, the oldest boys have started a logging business that requires hard work, skill, and a great deal of brains. Sitting in Bob's yard, the putt-putt of an engine one of the boys has recreated can be heard coming up the gravel road. One year, Skyler put together an assortment of steel pieces, rubber tires and a gasoline engine, building his own off road ATV. His proud smile through the smudges on his face is the same smile that he wears while courting a lovely young girl on the dance floor.

The Rusty Johnson family lives as one with their environment. Sitting in their living room, overlooking the yard, they count the deer wandering through, thinking that when the first of November rolls around, the hunting should be good. It is their policy that whatever game is taken is used. They do not kill for sport. A favorite picture is one of young Clay kneeling beside the first deer of the season.

I have learned to admire and respect the Rusty Johnson family because they have values and are virtuous in character. This makes them outstanding people. Rusty has a deep faith that he doesn't press on anyone. His belief is his and everyone else is free to have their own.

These values had to have come from somewhere. Anybody who has dealt with Rusty trusts his integrity, but the seed of his character was planted long before.

M Y WIFE CONVINCED ME I NEEDED to dress up to go to their wedding ceremony. Grudgingly I did that, and I was glad of it when I pulled our truck into the parking lot of the Trinity Lutheran Church of Hovland. My wife and I sat for a moment looking at the assortment of people threading their way into the small church. Built of stone and old pine it was a comforting sight, nestled among the towering pines surrounding it. This was the church where Kathi and Rusty first got married, with many of the same visitors attending again. A lot of Johnsons, Schuppels, and neighbors helped build it years ago.

Watching as people paired off exchanging greetings and smiles, I saw a sense of belonging. They truly belonged here, no matter what their religious connection. Groups of happy people crossing the gravel parking lot disappeared into the large double doors. Of special interest, a couple who seemed to know their way very well caught my attention. The man was dressed in a black suit and carried an air of distinction about him. The woman beside him had long gray hair flowing down her back, and she wore white boots. She had an elegant look to her, enough to stand out in any crowd. She wore a dress styled in the mid 1800s. It was elegant. With her companion in his black suit, the only word for the couple was *magnificent*.

At the entrance, everyone was greeted by the Reverend Kristin Garey, who seemed to know everyone, and knew what to say to each one. The ceremony was flawless and beautiful. As I watched the stature of Kathi and Rusty's three boys, CoLee, Skyler, and Clay; and listened to the golden voice of Bob's lovely daughter-in-law, Kelly, sing with Joy's son-in-law, Treg Axtell, I was sad to see the ceremony end. Usually, the agony of sitting through a wedding service was far from my personal choice, but that day I was captured by the sincerity of it. With Kelly's melodic tones still floating through my mind, I felt this was one of the most inspiring times I could remember.

The service over, everyone headed across the parking lot to the Hovland Town Hall for dinner.

The same band that had played at Bob's son Shawn's wedding with Kelly set up, while the rest of us ate. Kids ran around, people talked and laughed, and I came to think of us being in the center of one huge family.

The tables were cleared out and the lights lowered with the incredible sounds of the Rods & Reel band filled the small hall. I have to admit that I am not a polka dancer unless I'm incredibly drunk. Fortunately, there were only a few of those dances. As the evening wore on, the dignified man in the black suit and the magnificent woman in the old-fashion dress were on the floor a lot, floating in unison to whatever tune was being played. They danced as one. As I watched, I realized I had never seen two people move together so harmoniously.

I was compelled to ask Bob who they were and was told, "That's Rusty's parents."

It all came together for me. By witnessing the harmony of this lovely couple, I saw the accord that had instilled those wonderful traits in their children. I couldn't hold myself back; I had to talk to them. Hoping I wouldn't be intruding, I waited until the band took a break.

Mr. Johnson was reserved, though pleasant, and Mrs. Johnson reminded me of Queen Elizabeth and Eleanor Roosevelt all at once. With an extreme amount of poise and grace, Virginia Johnson gave me permission to attempt writing their story.

Duane and Virginia Johnson didn't do anything so extraordinarily different than so many other stalwart families who lived here. It's not just that they did it, but they did it with such . . . class.

T HE TINY TOWN OF HOVLAND is just a speck on the road to anyone driving north or south on Highway 61. Nestled at the bottom of a gentle valley, the few remaining buildings are just a blur to the tourists on their way to Duluth, the Grand Portage Casino, or to the Canadian border, a short twenty miles away. Hardly anyone who stops at Rydens Border Store will realize that a part of Hovland is sitting right in front of them, thanks to the industrious Duane Johnson. The quaint little Trinity Lutheran Church is often missed by passing traffic, as well as the concrete pier jutting out into Lake Superior, but the story behind these features is part of the Johnson legacy.

Racing across the shallow valley to get someplace else, nobody hears about the bank robbers caught in Hovland or the twenty-pound lake trout that still cruise the depths of the lake.

I feel sorry for travelers too inattentive to notice and stop at a small restaurant called, Chicago Bay Marketplace. There are a lot of eating places along almost every road, even Highway 61, but this one is special. The owner, Lisa Mesenbring, gets up before dawn each day to hand grind the wheat and rye that goes into the amazing breads she bakes. A hungry diner can relax with a good meal, a glass of fine wine or exotic beer, surrounded by photographs of early Hovland.

Just across the road is the unassuming home of Dusty Nelms and her family. Dusty, who was instrumental in providing information on her family, lives in the refurbished Mainella store and post office — the same one her mother worked in many years earlier.

South of Hovland sits the Naniboujou Lodge, rumored to be a hiding place for Al Capone early in its own history.

The many little stories that lie behind the scenery are missed by those hurrying to get someplace else. The new large homes overlooking the rugged Lake Superior shoreline indicate appreciation, but few of the people living in them understand the sacrifices and work that went into creating the little town of Hovland. No different than many other small Minnesota towns, perhaps, this is a close knit community. Everyone is welcomed and treated with dignity and respect by people with roots going back generations. However, the bonds between friends and relatives written into the history and growth of Hovland is special. Welcomed or not, to become a local takes generations of living, working, and sharing.

Driving home to Milaca with my wife, I talked about what I was planning, expressing doubts about doing the people of the North Shore justice. What could I write about that would be of interest to anyone? What was so special about these people and this area that compelled me to want to do this? After writing to Virginia, and reading their daughter Dusty's compilation of the things that Duane's family and Virginia's family had done to contribute to one of the most remarkable spots in Minnesota, it became obvious. The Johnson and Schuppel families have forged a part of history in the Arrowhead that needed telling. They are truly pioneers. *The salt of the earth.*

Chapter 3

The Development of the Johnson Family

Clarence Duane Johnson, b 16 June 1931, Duluth, Minnesota
Virginia Ann Schuppel, 9 May 1932, Grand Rapids, Minnesota

Married 14 February 1952, Hovland, Minnesota

~

Duane's maternal great grandfather:
Karl August Karlsson Sundqvist,
b- 6 March 1836, Pettböle, Finström, Aland
d- 2 June 1893, Pettböle, Finström, Aland
(son of Karl Gustav Johansson Sundqvist and Maja Brita Andersdotter)

Duane's maternal great grandmother:
Victoria Amanda Jonsdotter,
b- 11 April 1841, Bergon, Vardo, Aland
d- 24 July 1926, Pettböle, Finström, Aland
(daughter of Jonas Ersson and Maria Andersdotter)
Married 27 June 1869, Finström, Aland

~

Duane's paternal great grandfather:
Johan August Gabrielsson,
b- 13 Nov 1834, Galleryd, Kraksmala, Kalmar lan, Smaland, Sweden
date of death unknown, Kalmar lan, Smaland, Sweden
(son of Gabriel Gabrielsson and Magdalena Svensdotter)

Duane's paternal great grandmother:
Caroline Andersdotter,
b- 29 April 1831, Stora Granas, Madesjo, Kalmar lan, Smaland,
Sweden
date of death unknown, Kalmar lan, Smaland, Sweden
(daughter of Anders Petersson Granbom and Anna Maja Petersdotter)

Married 21 November 1860, Kristvalla, Kalmar lan, Smaland, Sweden

~

Duane's maternal grandfather:
August Werner Sundquist,
b- 1 August 1882, Pettböle, Finström, Aland
d- 31 January 1915, Hovland, Cook County, Minnesota
(son of Karl August Karlsson Sundqvist and Victoria Amanda
Jonsdotter)

Duane's maternal grandmother:
Anna Maria (Mary) Österbach,
b- 24 October 1883, Wassor Östman, Kvevlaks, Vaasa, Finland
d- 15September 1950, Hovland, Cook County, Minnesota
(daughter of Johan Wilhelm Österbach and Lisa Sofia Johansdotter Wast)

Married 26 December 1903, Eveleth, St. Louis County, Minnesota
~

Duane's paternal grandfather:
August Johnson
b- 23 November 1863, Stammeryd, Kristvalla, Kalmar lan, Smaland,
Sweden
d- 11 October 1926, Moose Valley, Hovland, Cook County,
Minnesota
(son of Johan August Gabrielsson and Caroline Andersdotter)

Duane's paternal grandmother:
Johanna Sofia Carlsdotter
(later known as Hanna Sofia Carlson)
b- 21 June 1873, Myoshyltan, Kraksmala, Kalmar lan, Smaland,
Sweden
d- 28 May 1948, Moose Valley, Hovland, Cook County, Minnesota

Married 3 July 1893, Cheboygan, Michigan

~

Duane's father:
Clarence August Johnson
b- 21 September 1905, Duluth, Minnesota
d- 9 November1992, Grand Marais, Minnesota
(son of August Johnson and Johanna Sofia Carlsdotter)

Duane's mother:
Ida Josephine Sundquist
b- 13 April 1907, Hovland, Minnesota
d- 16 January 1972, Duluth, Minnesota
(daughter of August Werner Sundquist and Anna Maria (Mary) Österbach)
Married 5 June 1929, Duluth, Minnesota

Clarence remarried 16 December, 1978 in Hovland, Minnesota to
Sylvia Matilda Carlson
b- 4 July 1906, in Eveleth, Minnesota
d 29 March 1991, Grand Marais, Minnesota
~

Virginia's maternal great grandfather:
Mathias Christensen Bergsven
b- 15 February 1833, Lilleulland, Faaberg, Oppland, Norway
d- 4 June 1917, Lessor Township, Polk County, Minnesota
(son of Christen Hansen Ulland and Marthe Pedersdotter)

Virginia's maternal great grandmother:
Mari Olsdotter Skaars-Eict
b- 14 January 1832, Skaars-Eict, Ostre Gausdal, Oppland, Norway
d- 23 June 1920, Pine Lake Township, Polk County, Minnesota
(daughter of Ole Johansen Skaarslien and Anne Olsdotter)

Married 18 June 1860, Ostre Gausdal, Oppland, Norway

~

Virginia's maternal grandfather:
Martin Bergsven
b- 17 November 1872, Vestre Gausdal, Oppland, Norway
d- 20 December 1956, Bemidji, Minnesota
(son of Mathias Christensen Bergsven and Mari Olsdotter)

Virginia's maternal grandmother:
Ida Maria Knoll Edwards
b- 17 February 1888, McIntosh, Minnesota
d- 9 February 1966, Bemidji, Minnesota
(daughter of Edward Eriksen Knoll and Lovise Olsdotter)
Married 25 June 1906, Crookston, Minnesota
~

Virginia's paternal great grandfather:
Johannes Schuppel
b- 27 January 1836, Kerchheim, Baden, Germany
d- 27 May 1920, Winona, Minnesota
(son of Friedrich W. Schuppel and Magdelena Kletti)

Virginia's paternal great grandmother:
Mary Muscovitz
b- 27 November 1841, Erfurt, Germany
d- 31 July 1917, Winona, Minnesota
(daughter of John Muscovitz and Mary Fisher)

Married 1859, Milwaukee, Wisconsin

~

Virginia's paternal grandfather:
John Schuppel
b- 3 October 1869, Stoddard, Wisconsin
d- 3 September 1937, Winona, Minnesota
(son of Johannes Schuppel and Mary Muscovitz)

Virginia's paternal grandmother:
Louise Wilhelmine Caroline Hahn (Minnie)
b- 23 February 1874, Fountain City, Wisconsin
d- 6 September 1951, Warroad, Minnesota
(daughter of C. F. G. Hahn and M. Willhelmine E. Langfeldt)

Married 23 June, 1897, Winona, Minnesota
~

Virginia's Father:
Harold Louis Willard Schuppel
b- 30 August 1902, Winona, Minnesota

d- 28 December 1964, Hovland, Minnesota
(son of John Schuppel and Louise Wilhelmine Caroline Hahn)

Virginia's Mother:
Leona Marie Bergsven
b- 27 August 1912, Grandview, Montana
d- 14 September 1981, Grand Marais, Minnesota
(daughter of Martin Bergsven and Ida Maria Knoll Edwards)

Married, 20 June, 1931, Bemidji, Minnesota

~

Duane & Virginia's children:
Sandra Jean Johnson b- 14 November 1952
Rocky Duane Johnson b- 25 January 1955
Dusty Lynn Johnson b- 2 November 1958
Stoney Lance Johnson b- 10 October 1960
Rusty Scott Johnson b- 20 March 1962
Misty Dawn Johnson b- 17 July 1964

Chapter 4

Duane's Maternal Grandparents
August Werner and Anna Marie Sundquist

Children: Oscar, born 24 May 1905
                    Ida Josephine, born 13 April 1907
                    Arthur Leonard, born 15 September 1910
                    John Oliver, born 9 August 1914

August Werner Sundquist

DUANE JOHNSON'S MATERNAL grandparents, Werner and Anna Maria Sundquist began the Johnson migration. The original spelling of "Sundquist" was "Sundqvist," and he was known by his middle name "Werner." He immigrated to America in 1900 at the age of eighteen. His older brother was in line to take over the family farm, so the journey to America was all but destined. Once here, he found work in the mines at Eveleth, Minnesota. If Werner settled in Eveleth, it can be assumed he worked at the underground mine at Fayal, near Eveleth.

The Fayal mine, entered by a vertical shaft, began in 1893 when rich deposits of iron ore were discovered by David T. Adams, of

19

Duluth. It was an extremely rich mine in the Mesabi range, which had many iron-ore deposits. In Eveleth the Johnson and Sundquist family legacy began.

Anna Maria Österbach

ANNA MARIA ÖSTERBACH'S HOME was Vasa Kvelax, Finland, which was a Swedish settlement just outside of Helsinki. Attending Swedish schools and churches, she wasn't exposed to the native Finnish language until she boarded the steamship for her trip to America.

At the age of eighteen, in 1901, Anna Maria told her parents she was leaving Finland to go to America, embarking on a pioneering adventure of her own. For a young girl to go off to a new country on her own took courage, but it was a life of opportunity she sought.

The common form of passage for peasants was to ride in steerage, being infinitely cheaper than state rooms. The hold of ships were often filled with families, primarily from Finland. With the extent of Anna Maria's understanding of Finnish being able to count to ten, she was at a disadvantage. Befriended by a Finnish family headed to Tennessee, she spent the journey in their company, leaning a lot in that time.

As with countless other immigrants, Ellis Island was her first view of America. Kept in a large cold building to wait for processing, she became separated from her adoptive family, and connected with a Swedish/Finnish family on their way to a place called Eveleth, Minnesota. The immigration official working with Anna bluntly told her that from now on, in America, she would be known as Mary.

With careless recording of names, such as Anna's, genealogy searches today are hampered by indiscriminate immigration entries.

On her arrival in America, Mary saw a vendor selling tomatoes and bought some. After tasting one, she thought they were terrible and threw them away. This was out of character for the frugal Mary.

In her new town of Eveleth, she took a job in a boarding house doing laundry, feeding babies, carrying milk cans, and scrubbing floors. Her hard work netted her $5.00 a month, working seven days a week. Accepting a different job at another boarding house for $10.00 a month, she quit that to become a nanny for a man with an invalid wife for $15.00 a month. While this work was cleaner and easier, it was located far into the countryside. She became despondent, with no other young people in the area, and yearned for a social life. At this point, a young and handsome, although quite wild, Werner met her, and she left to return to her job at the boarding house.

Werner and Mary

WITH HER MARRIAGE TO WERNER, December 26, 1903, Mary officially became an American citizen. Werner quickly discovered that the young and beautiful Mary had a few rules he had to heed. Succumbing to his love, his wild drinking days came to an end.

Tragedy struck the new family as Mary's first pregnancy ended with a miscarriage. A short time later, however, joy returned to the Sundquist family with the birth of little Oscar on May 24, 1905.

While working in the Eveleth mines, Werner became acquainted with Andrew Westerlund and Jacob Soderlund. His new friends were of Swede-Finn heritage also, so a close bond

August Werner Sundquist and Anna Maria Österbach, married December 26, 1903.

21

between the three families grew. Work in the mines was anything but satisfying; the men worked from daylight to dark under extremely dangerous conditions. Death and accidents in the mines were almost a daily occurrence. The most common related to explosions and cave-ins, falling down the deep vertical shaft, and being hit by tram cars. The only illumination in the mines between the years of 1860 to 1920 came from oil wick lamps.

In 1906 the three families made the decision to move on to a better and cleaner life. Information on Andrew Westerlund is vague, but Jacob Soderlund is recorded as having come from Esse, Finland. His daughter, Elsie Palmer, January 27, 1894 to November 29, 2004, is a contributor to some of the history presented in the Trinity Church chapter.

Mary Sundquist, Oscar, Art, Ida, and Oliver.

Mary and Werner Sundquist with Oscar and Ida.

Mary Sundquist at her spinning wheel.

August Werner and Anna Maria Sundquist, along with the Westerlunds and the Soderlunds, arrived at Hovland, Minnesota, on the shore of Chicago Bay, Lake Superior, in 1906. The Great Lakes steamship *America*, piloted by Captain Jacob F. Hector and Engineer Frank McMillan, was owned by Booth & Co., located in the Tribune Building in Chicago. The *America* was part of a fleet of vessels that serviced the North Shore, making a great impact on the success of settlers. At 185 feet, it was in service from 1902 until the spring of 1928 when it was lost at Isle Royale. For a while, the *America* was the only link to civilization for the residents of the North Shore.

Disembarking with their prized possession of one cow, the three families set out to homestead three available 160-acre sites in an area known as Poplar Hill, not far from the beautiful Brule River. To fairly choose who got which site, they drew matches.

The local hotel owner, Mr. Ellingsen, rented them a one-eyed horse to get their supplies to their new land. During construction of the first house, they stayed at the Bray family house, located one and one-half miles from the new home sites.

The Sundquist home was the first to go up, built from six-inch poplar logs. Mary and Mrs. Soderlund, each with a one-year-old child, moved into the finished home. They were kept busy snaring rabbits for food and tending to the daily rigors of their new life. The men needed an income, so took work at a logging camp at Portage Brook, twenty miles from the home sites. With no money for a horse, they walked the distance, to and from work.

After the Sundquist home, houses for the Soderlunds, then the Westerlunds were built.

Of all the potential dangers in her new surroundings, Mary feared horses the most. Their neighbors, the Rex family, were building a cabin nearby. Mary put Oscar in a buggy and strolled through the woods to visit the construction site. She could hear wolves howling, but that

Oscar, Art, Ida, Gramma Oliver, 1918.

Ida's first enterprize.

Ida and her cub.

didn't scare her. When she arrived at the site, to a man, the others casti-
gated poor Werner for letting his wife do such a careless thing.

The Sundquists built a second home in late 1909, near the original log home. This one was grander and finer than the poplar-log

Company at the farm.

Gramma and Grampa Sundquist, Ida,
and Oscar, 1909.

The second Sundquist home built in late 1909. Shown as it stands today on North Road.

home. This one had hardwood flooring and other components shipped in by boat. It was a fine framed home that even had a garage to house their first automobile, a Model T. One unsubstantiated story is that the new home was a pre-fab from Montgomery Ward. If this is true, it would have had to arrive by steam ship in Chicago Bay.

The Sundquist family was growing. With four children, Oscar, Ida, Arthur, and Oliver, their life, although difficult, was happy. They struggled through each day as it came and dealt with the problems they could tackle, leaving some to work out later or simply resolve.

However, tragedy struck the Sundqusits. August Werner Sundquist became afflicted with pneumonia while working at the logging camp. He died on December 31, 1915, at home.

Werner's obituary read: "He was a quiet man of few words, but a fine character and one of the most enterprising farmers in the community. He was a friend in need and always ready to lend a helping hand whenever opportunity presented itself."

August's untimely death at age thirty-three, just after Christmas in 1915, left Mary with four young children to raise on her own. In the rugged wilderness, survival for Mary and the children was a daily struggle. Oscar was just nine years old when he started working for a road crew, providing the family with their only income. Oscar's wages and the food they grew were all they had.

It is interesting to note that in 1978, Oscar was chosen as the year's Cook County Senior Citizen. His involvement in the community and propensity to help so many people made him an obvious choice. He was a president of the Grand Marais Lions Club, a member of the North Shore Hospital Board, and a board member of the Arrowhead Electric Cooperative. At the end of his accolades, a simple statement sums up Oscar to a tee. "He is a fine person to boot."

The family legacy to be resourceful, ethical and work hard and be available to others who need help, is a trademark.

Mary had no way to buy shoes, so she would knit tops and crochet them to the bottoms of old rubber boots to get them through the winter. The ever resourceful Oscar made a special crochet needle for his mother to make that job easier.

Oliver, Gramma, and Ida, 1921.

Mary had to spend her days working in the field, which left seven-year-old Ida to take care of four-year-old Arthur and six-month-old Oliver. Many years later, Ida would reflect on those times with the comment, "We worked like dogs."

In 1924, Mary went back to Finland to visit her family leaving Ida, age seventeen, to care for the family. Mary

HOMEMADE ICE CREAM* (1 gallon)

2 c. sugar   1 qt. whipping cream
Pinch salt   Milk
6 eggs, beaten
2 T. vanilla
Mix sugar, half of cream, vanilla, salt
and well beaten eggs together. Add
remainder of cream and mix well.
Pour into 1 gal. ice cream freezer, add
cold milk to fill 2/3 full. Freeze.

took a small amount of money and some jam for her mother. Mary had a sister, Ida, whom the daughter in America had been named after.

This Ida had a birth date of May 16, 1893, and she died on Febraury 12, 1951, in Vaasa, Finland. Evidently, her sister Ida was known as a spinster with a sever attitude, castigating Mary for taking food from her children. To Mary, jam was a special treat, having never tasted it until she got to America. She had only tasted one orange before her voyage as a young girl.

On her return to the family in Hovland, Mary had three copper teapots. She gave one each to Oscar, Ida, and Arthur.

Ida's industrious nature became obvious when she and a friend, Anne, started a business near her home called Poplar Booth. They sold ice cream, pop, and candy, and Ida's pet bear cub attracted a lot of attention at the store.

Edwin Sannes
May 12, 1891 to November 9, 1945

SINCE WERNER'S DEATH in 1915, Mary did everything possible to keep her family healthy, safe, and happy. On September 26, 1927, over twelve years after Werner's passing, Mary and a Norwegian man named Ed Sannes got married. Few facts on Ed are available, but aside from being a fisherman, he was an industrious man doing well with property. Ed was a fishing partner with Nels Norman. Nels bought some Big Bay property from Bernt Jacobson, and Ed in turn, bought the property from Nels in 1927.

Over time, Ed held property on the Lake Superior shore, in Big Bay, Moose Valley, and Chicago Bay. Ed and Mary's home site was the property on Lake Superior, between Hovland and what is now Judge C.R. Magney State Park. They had a daughter, Helen.

In an interview with Arthur for a family gathering in 1995 when he was eighty-five-years old, he offered many recollections. When he was about twelve years old, probably in the year 1922, the old log cabin they had built first burned down. The fire spread to the wood-shed, which housed their Model T, the first family car, destroying everything. The Soderlund family teamed up with the Sundquists, helping save the home.

The home is still standing on North Road, vacant and unassuming. Weeds are growing up around it, and time had has its deterioratory effect. The Sundquist family lived in it and rose each morning to face another day. Enduring the death of Werner, the family did what they had to do.

Chapter 5

Duane's Paternal Grandparents
August and Hanna Sophia Johnson

Children: Andrew Robert, born 27 March 1892
Johann Albin, born 16 June 1894
Amy Aleda, born 2 September 1896
John Arthur, born 12 October 1899
Charles William, born 17 December 1901
Clyde Ernest, born 20 June 1903
Clarence August, born 21 September 1905
Mildred Marguerite, born 16 January 1908

August Johansson

AUGUST JOHANSSON WAS BORN on November 23, 1863, in the small village of Stammeryd, Kristvalla Parish, Kalmar lan, Småland, Sweden. He was the son of Johan Gabrielsson, a laborer, and Karoline Andersdotter. As a young man, August also worked as a laborer at Kristvalla, as well as training in the Swedish military in 1884 and 1885.

At this time, mass emigration from Sweden was taking place. The major causes for the movement were primarily land and job

August Johansson (changed to Johnson).

August Johnson and Johanna Sofia Carls-dotter, married July 3, 1893.

opportunities in America. Transportation had also improved. In particular, Kalmar lan experienced a heavy migration at this time. The idea that his dreams could be fulfilled apparently ignited the wanderlust in August. He received official permission to leave Kristvalla on June 28, 1888, with his destination either New York or Boston. With the help of someone in America, he was sent a ticket for passage, leaving from Malmo, Sweden, on July 12, 1888, aboard the steamer *Oresund* of the Cunard line.

The usual route traveled by most Swedish emigrants at the time was to go by ship from Malmo to the English port of Hull, then by rail to Liverpool. After a delay of several days, the ten- to twelve-day sea journey from Liverpool to America began. From his arrival in August 1888, August Johansson made his way to Cheboygan, Michigan. It is

31

Certificate of citizenship for August Johnson, September 11, 1896.

The original Johnson family home in Moose Valley. Left to right: August, Mildred, Hanna, Art, Clyde, Clarence Johnson, Cousin Gus Person, and Charlie Johnson.

The original Johnson family home in Moose Valley. Left to right: the family dog, "Ring," Art (kneeling next to Helen Udclaire), Clyde, Millie, Clarence, and Charlie Johnson.

August Johnson with his oxen at Moose Valley.

not known for certain, but there is a strong possibility that August had to work his way along the route.

33

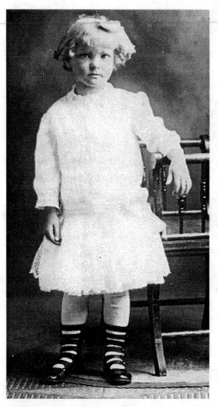

Millie Johnson at about three or four years.

Once in Cheboygan, August was able to find work in sawmills and in the logging industry. The reputation of the Swedish immigrants was one of good hard workers, in spite of the language barriers. Typical sawmills where August could have found work were, Vyn Sawmill, operated by a Scandinavian named, Geert Vyn and the Brouwer & Vos Sawmill. Many of these enterprises were started in an economic boom and were later sold to larger companies or burned down and closed forever. Cheboygan's first sawmill was built in 1846, lasting through a sixty-year economic boom. When the timber business slowed, many workers left to find work in more lucrative areas, August among them.

Johanna Sofia Carlsdotter

JOHANNA SOFIA, WAS BORN on June 21, 1873, in the village of Myoshyltan, Kraksmala Parish, Kalmar lan, Småland, Sweden. Her parents were Karl Johan Johanson and Anna Gustafva Nilsdotter, and she had a twin sister, Thilda Maria.

Johanna received official permission to leave Kraksmala Parish on August 9, 1889, at the young age of sixteen. She left with her older sister, Wendla, and her husband Jacob and daughter Anna. Taking the typical route through Hull and Liverpool, they eventually landed in New York. From there, they traveled to Cheboygan, where

Clarence and Mildred Johnson with the Moose Valley School in the background.

Johanna worked for an English family. She soon mastered the English language by reading the newspapers, books, and magazines in the home.

August and Hanna

AUGUST AND HANNA, as Johanna was now called, had known each other in Sweden, so it was inevitable after they met again that they should marry. The wedding took place on July 3, 1893. They had four children in Cheboygan: Andrew Robert, born March 27, 1892; Johann Albin, born June 16, 1894; Amy Aleda, born September 2, 1896; and John Arthur, born October 12, 1899. Johann, however, at age three, died of scarlet fever.

A typical farm scene at the Moose Valley School: Left to right: N.J. Bray, Mildred Johnson, Clarence Johnson, Clyde Johnson, Charles Johnson, and Pete Peterson, October 6, 1913.

Millie playing the accordion with her music partner, Lefty.

The Moose Valley School, October 3, 1913. Left to right: Pete Peterson, Charlie Johnson, N.J. Bray (teacher), Clyde Johnson, and Clarence Johnson.

August, who had now Americanized his name to Johnson, became an official citizen of the United States on September 11, 1896.

In 1900, August moved his family from Cheboygan to Duluth, Minnesota, where he worked in the sawmills. During the winter months, he would take a boat north to Hovland to work in the logging camps. Then in the springtime he would walk one hundred miles back to Duluth to rejoin his family. That sounds like a daunting task today, but as with Werner Sundquist, Andrew Westerlund, and Jacob Soderlund, walking twenty miles to work every day, it was simply what needed to be done.

In Duluth, four more children were born to August and Hanna: Charles William, born December 17, 1901; Clyde Ernest, born June 20, 1903; Clarence August, born September 21, 1905; and Mildred Marguerite (Millie), born January 16, 1908. Tragedy struck the family again when sixteen-year-old Andrew Robert was accidentally electrocuted while playing with some boys. He had climbed a power pole and touched a live wire on April 14, 1908. He is buried at the Oneota Cemetery in Duluth.

August Johnson earned his living at the logging camps in Hovland, so, after several years of commuting from Duluth, he built a log cabin there. His family arrived in Hovland on July 9, 1910, aboard the steamship *America*. He met them at the dock with horse and wagon, bringing them to their new home in Moose Valley. The patent for the homestead was received August 29, 1916.

The family cleared sixty acres of land, by hand, for farming. They raised potatoes, carrots, and other vegetables. The chickens all had names relating to neighbors in the area, such as "Julia" or "Jenny." Eventually, as many as eight cows gave them enough butter and cream to be able to sell some to a nearby store in Hovland. Millie, at four years old, had a white calf she would play with and treat as a pet, like most kids would do with a dog.

After the Johnsons moved to Moose Valley, a small school was built to accommodate them and their cousins, the Peterson children. Built of hand-hewn logs like his house was, August covered the exterior with boards painted red with white trim. The one-room country school house had a big round wood stove in the corner. Hannah, living across from the school, would get the stove fired up in the morning, and clean it before classes started. In the beginning, a female teacher, probably Clara Borg, lived above the school and ate at the Johnson home. In the house with six children already, feeding another person became an additional burden, but this was accepted happily.

In an article written by Barb Hirsch about Mildred (Millie) Johnson Mainella for a church column called "Meet a Parishoner," Millie recounts her life in Moose Valley: "The only pupils in the school were the six children from my family and the Peterson children. They were John, Charles, Gustaf, Peter, Annie, and Eva. In 1911 the Moose Valley School closed as there weren't enough left to keep it open. My brothers, Clyde and Clarence, and I, went to school in Hovland. My brother Clyde finished that school the first year, and Clarence and I stayed with the Ellingson's until we finished.

"The Ellingsons were Norwegian and very nice people. They could only speak Norwegian, and as we were Swedish, it did take awhile before we could understand them very well. Mr. Ellingson had the only store in Hovland at that time. Their house was also the boarding house in the community, and people who got off the steamer *America*, would stay there. In those days the only two modes of transportation were the steamer or dog sled.

"The Ellingson house was also the post office, which was located in their sitting room. Our teacher, Mr. Bray, also served as the postmaster at that time. The mailman, Emil Hall, and his family lived in a couple rooms upstairs of the Ellingson house. Mail was not delivered every day in those days. It came by horse team only once or twice a week.

"I was only about ten years old when I first stayed at the Ellingsons; Clarence was about twelve years old. We would walk home to Moose Valley on weekends and return Sunday afternoon. One weekend Clarence was somewhere else, so I walked alone. As I started up the road from Big Bay (where a family by the name of Olsen lived), I walked about a half mile up the road before I heard wolves howling. I turned around and ran as fast as I could to get back to the Olsens. They were just eating their supper, but Mr. Olsen lit a kerosene lamp and walked me the three miles to our house. So, he walked six miles that night, just for me. I often think what a nice person he was.

"I remember my teacher, Miss Borg, also, as a special person. She and I both had upstairs rooms in the Ellingson house. Her room was right next to mine. I had never been alone at night before as I always slept with my mother. I had trouble falling asleep so I would pound on the wall and say, 'Miss Borg, may I come and sleep with you? I can't sleep.' She would always say, 'Yes, come in.' I shall never forget her and I wonder if she ever thought I was a pesky kid.

"Everyone in those days lived off the land, you might say. We planted and raised our own vegetables, picked our own fruit—raspberries, strawberries, blueberries and cranberries, which were all canned, as there was no refrigeration in those days. One summer my mother picked and canned 100 quarts of strawberries right from our own field. She wouldn't quit until she had canned that many. I remember stemming all those berries, which didn't make me very happy!

"My brother Art shot his first moose right from our back door when he was twelve years old. He later became a game warden, a position he held for forty-two years. He was the oldest of my living brothers. My only sister, Amy, was two years older than Arthur, and she got married at the age of sixteen and lived in Duluth. My niece, Helen, was born when Amy was seventeen years old, so that made me an aunt when I was five years old. As a result, Helen and I were very close emotionally—more like sisters. She has two sons and one daughter—all of whom are married and have families.

"One summer my mother, Clyde, and Clarence went blueberry picking, so Amy, Charlie, and I were at home. That day I wanted to help Charlie milk our cow. I ran through the tall grass looking for the stool to sit on. There was a broken bottle hidden in the grass, which I didn't see. I was barefoot and stepped on a very jagged piece, which cut an artery in my left foot. I almost fainted as the bleeding couldn't be stopped. Amy knew there was a man by the name of Asa Hoyt who was a nurse, and he happened to be haying at the Peterson farm next to our place. Amy told Charlie to get him quickly, which he did. He told Amy that it was a good thing she asked for his help, as I could have bled to death. He made a tourniquet to put around my ankle and elevated my foot, which stopped the bleeding. I had to keep my foot elevated for several days. Even when I started school that fall I couldn't wear a shoe so I went limping around in stocking feet on my heel.

"We only had one cow for many years, but she kept us in milk and butter. She had calves, which I loved to play with, and they were so cute. Eventually our herd grew.

"When Mr. Bray taught school in Hovland, he liked to put on programs. Most parents thought he spent too much time doing that, and they objected. This one time none of the parents or the children showed up for the program. I had learned every one's part as I had listened carefully when they practiced. So, I did the whole program, including the songs and loved every minute of it. There wasn't much of an audience, as most of the parents who had children in school, along with the children, did not attend. The teacher, Mr. Bray, was also the local postmaster during World War I and sold thrift stamps at the post office, so he gave me a thrift stamp for doing the program. The thrift stamp was used to purchase. We kept them in a book until enough stamps had been collected to purchase a savings bond, which helped the First World War effort. Many years afterwards whenever there was a gathering of people in the area he would re-tell this story.

"For many years we didn't have horses, so my mother would walk to the Bay (which was Hovland) for groceries and carry them home in a pack sack on her back. I would tag along and carry what I could. She would hire someone who had a team of horses to haul the heavy things like flour and sugar, which she bought in 100# sacks. She used a lot of flour as she baked her own bread (eight loaves at a time), as there were eight or more people at the table for each meal. She did all of this with an old cast-iron wood-burning stove, but I shall never forget the good bread and rolls.

"For washing clothes, she would catch rain water in the summer, and in the winter she would melt snow. As there was no washing machines in those days, she washed all the clothes by using an old scrub board and did everything by hand. All of the water was heated on the stove, and all the white things were placed in a large boiler and boiled on the stove to keep them white. Everything had to be hung outside to dry (even in the winter when they would freeze stiff as a board) but they really smelled nice and fresh when they were brought into the house.

"For drinking water, we had a hand-dug well. We used this water for the livestock, too. When we didn't have enough rain, we used this water for laundry, but it was hard water and wasn't as good for cleaning the clothes as rain water.

"The Peterson family grew up and left the valley, so the farm has been vacant for many years. Some people would come in and cut the hay, and sometimes people would camp there when they would go hunting. Now there are some beautiful homes built there.

"One Christmas our Hovland School and the North School (which was back on the North road) put on their Christmas program together. Our teacher was Clara Borg, and we children would walk about six miles each way to practice for our program. The evening of the program, we all got rides from the families who had horses. Our neighbor, Mr. Ellquist, who lived in the valley, had a team of horses and would let us ride with him. He had sleigh bells on the horses, and we would sing Christmas songs as we drove along to school and back home after the program. What fun that was! We would get back up the valley at the wee hours of the morning as the program was held at the North School, which was at least ten miles from the valley. That school has been gone for years, and the one in Hovland has been re-built a couple of times.

"The roads in those days were not good. In the winter we would have to ski or snowshoe to get places. My brother Charlie made all of our skis, sleds, and snowshoes, and he became quite a craftsman. Making snowshoes is a lot of work. He would use the hide from the deer he killed for our food. He would tan the hide, then cut it in strips, and these strips were then woven into the snowshoe frame which he made also. Skis were not quite as much work but he made them so they worked very well.

"After a while we got a team of horses which we used to do the heavy chores around the farm and to get our groceries. I thought it was great fun to go horseback riding on them also. Then later on we got our first Model-T Ford car. Clarence did most of the driving. Sometimes when it was low on gas, he would turn around and drive it backwards up the Moose Valley hills as the gas would run back into the tank and not reach the motor if he continued driving forward. That about covers my memories of growing up in Hovland which I enjoyed in spite of the hardships."

SCHOOL WAS AN IMPORTANT PART of the lives of not only the children, but the adults. Seeing that their children received an education was essential to their development and the development of the area. From the beginning, it was important to build the school and provide housing for the teacher. Children were sometimes boarded in town, as well when weather or distance from the school were issues. There was a close bond in the community between the church and school; this is evident even today. It would seem that Mr. Bray's efforts at staging school programs did reach a limit for the hard-working families, who staged a gentle protest.

A project carried on by schools at that time was known as an "Industrial County." The purpose was to interest children in the arts of wood working, growing gardens, cooking, and sewing. Young Charlie Johnson won first prize with a model of a log cabin he built.

Mr. Bray encouraged the Moose Valley students to learn how to grow various crops in their school garden. In the fall of 1912, a portion of the schoolyard was plowed in preparation for the following spring. They planted emmer, rye, wheat, clover, Canada pea, magel beets, and potatoes.

To the pride of the children, the September 8, 1913, issue of the *Cook County News Herald*, stated, "Moose Valley School celebrated the first day with boiled sweet corn raised in its own experimental garden for dinner. Each school day since it has indulged in a different variety of garden food of its own raising including potatoes, fresh peas, lettuce, carrots, rutabagas, and is already planning for a Thanksgiving pumpkin pie of its own."

The Johnson kids were isolated at Moose Valley, so they provided their own entertainment. Years later, Clyde recalled, "Whenever we had time between work, like weeding the garden, picking berries, helping with haying or other chores, we went fishing or skiing in the winter, or trapping. We made our own skis. One year, one of the teachers gave all of us boys each a pair of skis. They were made of yellow pine so they didn't last long. We also built shacks. We even built one up in some trees. We also played scrub baseball, which only required three or four to play."

Most of the Johnson family liked to run. Hannah, Clarence, and Millie went to a lot of races, usually winning. Clyde said, "Clarence always wanted to be first at whatever he did."

After clearing the Moose Valley land by hand in order to homestead, Duane's grandfather, August, set out hand-hewing railroad ties with a broad axe for the railroads before they started sawing them. His reputation with the broad axe was known throughout the area as he became very good at it. He built their first home in Moose Valley with hewn logs.

August worked on roads in the Hovland area during the summer, walking both ways to work, fourteen miles each day. Clyde said about his father, "August moved at a slower pace, but he did a good job and got the job done."

After a year-long battle with stomach cancer, at the age of sixty-two, August Johnson died on Monday, October 11, 1926, at home in Moose Valley.

Soon after the death of August, Hannah and her family moved into their new home at Moose Valley. A white clapboard house with a porch on the front, it was located towards the end of Moose Valley Road. At this writing, the house is still standing.

Recollections from one of Hannah's granddaughters: "We thought the house was huge with a big roomy kitchen where Grandma was always cooking, baking or canning. When we went to visit, she always had fresh bread or cookies for us. She would take us out to the chicken coop with her to gather eggs, shooing the hens off their nests. When they started flapping their wings and flying around, I would duck and run screaming from the coop."

Hannah Johnson passed away at her home in Moose Valley on May 28, 1948. She had been ailing for a number of months and suffered a stroke about two weeks before her death. Both August and Hannah are buried at the Trinity Lutheran Church cemetery in Hovland.

For many years after Hanna's death, rumors of her house being haunted were passed from one person to another. Whether or not Hanna came back, one story has to make a person curious.

At one time, Hanna's house was rented out. Shortly thereafter, the renters said they couldn't live there anymore. A mystical presence was seen in the kitchen. The woman was shown a picture of Hanna, with her excitedly exclaiming, "Yes, that's who I saw. That's her."

Later in life, when Amy Aleda was asked how she kept herself busy, she said, "As for activity, there wasn't much in those days. My mother worked, and I was left in charge of the home, with four brothers and a baby sister to take care of, and I helped with the house work. When we moved to Moose Valley, there was plenty of work to do. If we wanted to attend anything we had to walk."

Amy became good friends with Jennie Ojard, another Hovland girl, and they went to quite a few school programs and dances together. Amy moved to Duluth where she worked at the wholesale house of Wright and Clarkson, until she got married to "Charlie" Udclaire, on November 30, 1912. When their two children, Helen and Robert, were old enough to travel, the family would embark onto the *America* to Hovland to visit family and friends. The trip usually took all day, and sometimes until midnight. Later, when the Johnson's bought their first car, an old Ford, they would drive to Duluth to pick them up. However, that usually took all day also.

John Arthur "Art" Johnson's official birth record gives October 12, 1899, as the date, but Art insisted it was October 1st. So, that's the date he would recognize. He helped his father on the farm until he took a job as wheelsman on the Great Lakes ships operating then. He held this position for seven to eight years. Art's brother Clyde recalled, "When Art shot his first moose right out the front door of our log home in Moose Valley, he was just twelve, and the moose was about half a mile away." Clyde added, "When Art later became a game warden, he was a good at it because he knew what to look for." Art provided most of the meat and brook trout for the family, with his mother, Hanna, canning most of it. In the spring of 1924, Joe Brickner became the Cook County game warden, and he encouraged Art to become a state warden. Art accepted. He and Charles Ott held that position until the time of Art's death in 1965.

On July 9, 1930, Art married Minnie Vog in Warroad. Minnie graduated from Moorehead State College and started teaching in 1927. She proudly taught school for thirty-two years, twenty-nine of them in Grand Marais. Art and Minnie had two children, Robert and Margaret, but little Robert died right after he was born.

CLYDE ERNEST JOHNSON WORKED with Walter Nelson and Charlie Peterson in a logging camp near Swamp River around 1920. They floated logs down the Swamp River to the Pigeon River, then on to Lake Superior. In 1921, Clyde worked at his Uncle Charlie Johnson's logging camp in Colville. He hauled logs from the camp down to the shore of Lake Superior, where they would be rafted across the lake in the spring. In the winter, Clyde loaded the logs on a sleigh to bring them down to the lake. In between logging jobs, Clyde worked on town roads, later taking over the family farm.

On June 18, 1950, Clyde married a fascinating woman, Eileen Laura Kelly, in Duluth. The wedding date was not picked at random, as Eileen's great-grandmother, her great aunt, and her mother had all gotten married on that same date. Eileen received a B.E. degree from Duluth State Teachers College, (which is now U.M.D.) in 1934. She taught one year in North Dakota, and two years in Hovland, where she met Clyde. She also taught in high schools at Esko, Kimball, Bemidji, Grand Marais, and Barnum. In addition to teaching, Eileen was involved in Girl Scouts, often having ten to twelve Scouts up to the farm. The impish side of Eileen came out when she would sneak up on the girls, asleep in the hayloft, and scare the living daylight out of them. To calm them down, she would ad lib ghost stories for the rest of the night.

Eileen had a collection of at least a hundred dolls from different parts of the world. Bobbi, her niece, fondly recalls the gift of miniature dolls given to her and Charlene at Christmas. Eileen sewed intricate wedding dresses for the dolls that resembled an old fashioned wedding dress from a picture of Grandmas wedding.

Clyde's niece, Bobbi (Johnson) Lord gives us an intimate look at Clyde, saying, "Uncle Clyde stayed on the farm and helped out Grandma (Hannah Johnson) after all the other kids had left to raise their own families. He would take us out to the barn with him and let us watch him milk the cows. I don't know how many head he had to milk, but once in a while he would squirt milk at us. He even let us try to milk the cows, but I never got the hang of that. After the milk was collected in buckets, he would take it down to the basement of the farmhouse and process it. It was fascinating to watch him separate the milk from the cream and then churn the cream into butter. He filled up bottles of milk and sold them to the stores."

Bobbi goes on with, "After Grandma died, Uncle Clyde would come down and have dinner with us on Sundays and then take us for a ride; maybe up to the border or someplace. One winter, on a Saturday night, Charlene and I wanted to go to Grand Marais to the theater to see *Samson and Dehlila*. It was the last night they were showing it, but the problem was that there was a blizzard blowing, and Dad would not drive in it with the Model A. Mom called Uncle Clyde, and he came down and picked us up in the small school bus. It took forever, it seemed, to get to Grand Marais from Hovland and back home again, but we made it. Uncle Clyde always came through for us."

From my view point, it would seem that Clyde was the kind of uncle that everyone would want. Always involved in the community, Clyde and his brother Charlie, helped to build the Hovland Town Hall.

Eileen passed away February 17, 1989, and Clyde passed on peacefully in his sleep on October 20, 1996.

CHARLES WILLIAM JOHNSON was a typical Johnson in that he became a part of his community and the natural surroundings he lived in. In the mid 1930s he was a foreman at CCC camps, and was associated with Consolidated Paper and Diamond Tool in Duluth. However, his lifetime work was with the Cook County Highway Department, where he worked for twenty-six years. His daughter Bobbi describes Charley as, "A nice-looking man with curly hair."

The Johnson trait of being a craftsman was repeated in Charlie. Skilled at woodworking, he made a toboggan and a couple sets of skis for the kids, as well as a wooden boat used for many years. Along with adding a second story to the house, he helped build the Hovland Town Hall, which is still in use today. Charlie also made several pairs of snowshoes, being one of the last people who really knew how to weave the hide on the frames. Bobbi remembers using them when they went out looking for the Christmas tree. Now, son George Johnson has them adorning his living room wall.

Charlie's method of fishing was a little different from the typical way. He would walk up Carlson's Creek and shoot the fish with a .30-.30. Ironic since his brother Art was a game warden.

On Christmas day 1933, Charlie married Mabel Stormoen at Bagley, Minnesota. Mabel was a school teacher in Hovland for three years, where she and Charlie met. Their home was located at the corner where Moose Lake Road meets Highway 61 and commanded a nice view of Lake Superior.

Mabel was adept at sewing clothes for the children, where summertime Saturdays were spent creating skirts with Bobbi and Charlene to wear to dance at the town hall. Mabel was an accomplished musician, entertaining the family with singing and teaching some of them to play the piano. With all her talents, one outstanding feature about Mabel is that she loved to read. She had a collection of books that helped get the children through countless book reports. She was also writer of the Hovland news column for the Grand Marais paper, for years. A first class cook, Bobbi recalls the yearly ritual of making blood sausage, even after her boyfriend saw her with the beef blood covering her arms. According to Bobbi, "He turned white, then green, and left real fast."

Charlie passed away on November 11, 1971, and Mabel died September 26, 1968.

Mildred Marguerite Mainella (Millie), Duane's aunt, was born January 16, 1908, in Duluth. Her story is especially interesting as it illustrates the economic hardship that people faced as a daily routine. Her accounting in the church article appears earlier in this chapter.

Moving to Moose Valley, in Hovland, at the age of two, Mildred eventually attended school there. After the Moose Valley School closed, she attended the Chicago Bay School until the eighth grade. To attend high school would mean moving to Grand Marais, which was impossible at the time. Instead, she took a business course at the Duluth University, staying with her older sister, Amy.

There were no jobs available in Cook County, so she went to Beaver Bay to operate a switchboard for five years. That, combined with work as a waitress, she earned $30.00 a month plus room and board. After a new owner took over the switchboard, she left the waitress work and helped sort mail in the post office. Next was a two-year stint in Duluth as a housekeeper, as her inexperience kept most jobs out of her reach. An occasional gig playing the accordion for dances lined her up with the Werner Noreen and Herman Webber bands.

On one of her trips back to Hovland, she met Charlie Mainella, who had came to Hovland in 1938 with a CCC group and ran a small lunch room serving sandwiches and pie. At the time, a whole pie sold for a dollar, and a single slice was ten cents. One had to sell a lot of pies to make a living.

Charles Mainella became good friends with Charlie Johnson, Millie's brother. Charlie brought Mainella home with him, and he was introduced to Millie, who was on one of her trips home. She said

Millie's husband, Charles Roxie Mainella.

she wasn't too impressed — he didn't dance, and she loved dancing. Millie said that after she got to know him, she found that he wasn't such a bad guy after all.

Love intertwined, and they were married June 24, 1941, in Duluth. Charlie's family had an interesting background. His father, Carl, was born in Italy in 1848, shortly before the family immigrated. Charlie's grandfather, Joseph Russo, was a musician who played the harp. When Joseph was young, he traveled from town to town playing in dance halls and saloons with two friends. Charlie recalled Joseph, before the Civil War, walking from Brainerd to Duluth over oxen trails and through swamps to play with his two companions. The stunning feature to this was that he walked from Duluth to St. Paul with his harp and haversack on his back.

Carl traveled to Canada, then Duluth, in 1871. After a time of cooking on boats on the Great Lakes, Charlie came back to Hovland to run a grocery store and gas station. In 1945, Charlie turned down an offer to become the postmaster in Hovland, turning it over to Millie for $50.00 a month. The post office was located in the store, which is now the home of Duane and Virginia's daughter, Dusty.

The first years Mainella owned the store, he sold on credit. Times were tough, and there was no money coming in. The store was closed, and Charles went to work in Alaska driving truck. Returning from Alaska, the store was reopened, and they ran it until he retired in 1971. Charles Mainella was an astute business man, making good deals on property on Tom Lake. He later sold off parcels, turning a good profit. Charlie passed away December 16, 1977, in Grand Marais.

One of the highlights in Millie's life was a Lawrence Welk concert in Duluth, where she danced with the famous musician.

On Millie's recent birthday she received notoriety in a newspaper article. When asked about the secret to leading such a long life, she said, "Lead a clean life, take care of your health, try to stay happy and think positively. When you start thinking negatively say, 'Get behind me!' You're going to have good and not so good days, but don't expect anything different."

At this moment, Millie is a very proud 101 years of age. My deepest thanks are extended to Barb Hirsch for recording so many details of Millie's life in the "Meet A Parishioner" column.

Chapter 6

Duane's Parents
Clarence August and Ida Josephine Johnson

Children: Clarence Duane, born 16 June 1931
Carol Jeanette, born 22 September 1939
Arline Faye, born 29 April 1941

Clarence August Johnson

Clarence August was five-years old when the steamer America, docked at Hovland, in 1910, settling in at Moose Valley. He attended school there until 1917, when it was closed. At age twelve, he started school at Chicago Bay, in Hovland, but had to board at Ellingsen's Hotel. His teachers were N. J. Bray, Adeline Berglund, and Clara Borg. As was the necessity of most youngsters at the time, Clarence worked on the farm all through school, until turning sixteen in the eighth grade. A hard working farm boy, he had a love for entertainment, also. An accomplished accordion player, he would walk for miles to attend, and play at, dances.

After finishing school, he worked in a lumber camp skidding out logs, using only horses for power. Next, Clarence became a road boss for the town of Hovland. Truck driving was his next ambition, working for the Highway Department in 1927 and 1928. May 1, 1929, was a memorable one for Clarence, marking the start of his job for the Forestry Department, working during the summer until 1937. In the fall and early spring he would do commercial fishing. In 1937 he became a full-time employee for Minnesota Forestry, ending his career on September 30, 1970, after forty-one years of service.

Clarence's forty-one years in forestry entailed roadwork, timberwork, cruising and scaling timber, and sundry other jobs. He said, of his work, "I liked the work, it was okay." When asked if he would do it all over again, he said he would. He added, "The first years were much more to my liking, because the work was done out in the field. In the last years, it was mostly sitting in the office, and you almost had to be a collage graduate to handle the reports."

The new Johnson home at Moose Valley. Left to right: Millie, Hannah, Amy, Clarence, and Clyde Johnson.

Ida (Sundquist) and Clarence Johnson.

At Clarence's retirement he received awards from Governor LeVander and the Forestry Department.

WHEN THE SUNDQUIST, Westerlund, and Soderlund families arrived in 1906, and the Johnson family arrived in 1910, they docked at a wooden pier at Hovland.

At about the age of sixteen or seventeen, around 1921, Clarence was involved in rebuilding the dock to the concrete platform that still stands in the harbor today. Camping in a tent on the shoreline all summer, Clarence had the job of helping to haul sand in a barge pulled by an old motor boat. The sand was needed to mix with the cement and came from the site that is now occupied by the Naniboujou Lodge, a journey of about three miles. One of these trips stood out in Clarence's mind. The tow boat made an unexpected turn with the tow rope catching him and pitching him overboard. There was no such thing as life jackets in those days, so he treaded water while the tow boat and barge slowly circled around to pick him up. At that time of the year, the water temperature could reach fifty degrees. Being in the water was very dangerous.

The large concrete pier Clarence helped build is a landmark in Hovland.

At one time, a logging camp in Moose Valley was located by Carlson's Creek and near where Highway 61 is today. Clarence and his brother Charlie were hunting, passing through the old camp, when they came upon the body of a man hanging by a rope. This experience was also not something very easily forgotten.

Clarence August and Ida Josephine

ON JUNE 5, 1929, CLARENCE married Ida Josephine Sundquist in Duluth. Ida and Clarence probably knew each other growing up, but didn't become close until they were in their teens. Ida went to the North School, living in Poplar Hill; and Clarence attended the Chicago Bay School, living in Moose Valley. At the end of the school year, the two schools would have a picnic together, giving Clarence and Ida a chance to meet informally. The new couple made their home on the shores of Lake Superior. The always industrious Ida wasn't ready to settle down. She started a small cabin rental business, doing quite well with it. It gave Ida a great deal of pleasure making her renters happy, with camp fires on the beach and picnics. Nearby neighbors and other families would join, with a grand time for everyone.

Ida didn't get out fishing too often, but when a chance came, she enjoyed it very much. The church was an ever-present object in their lives, with Ida active in the church activities, being treasurer for many

Left to right: Clyde Johnson, Ed Sannes, Mary (Sundquist) Sannes, Helen Sannes, Hannah Johnson, Art Johnson, Helen Udclair, and Millie Johnson.

Game warden Art Johnson at his retirement with commendation by Governor C. Elmer Anderson.

years. The Ladies Aid was a project she was very close to, as it was her nature to help others whenever she could. One can look back on the responsibilities she had as a young girl taking care of her family to see what she was like as an adult.

As well as her philanthropic efforts, Ida was known for the good food she cooked. The children knew she would always have cookies ready for them whenever they would pop into her kitchen. A favorite was the marshmallows dipped in chocolate.

Ida passed away January 16, 1972, in Duluth, being buried at Trinity Lutheran Church cemetery in Hovland. Years later, on December 16, 1978, Clarence married Sylvia Matilda Carlson in Hovland, moving to a residence in Grand Marais.

Sylvia passed away March 29, 1991; followed by Clarence on November 9, 1992.

Charles Johnson with his accordion.

Chapter 7

Duane Johnson

I
F RUSTY JOHNSON IS DEEMED to be resourceful it is a trait he inherited from his father, Duane. It has now become obvious that the family legacy is passed from one generation to the next. Seeing resourcefulness in Rusty and Kathi's children is testament to parents who took the time and effort to install it properly.

CLARENCE DUANE JOHNSON was born June 16, 1931, in Duluth, and lived on the Sundquist farm until he was six. His parents bought a house built by his step-grandfather, located next to Lake Superior, in Hovland.

Duane's closest friends were Lloyd Norman and Kenneth Koss. Both of their fathers were commercial fishermen, which became Duane's future dream. The fascination of the vastness of Lake Superior, loomed in front of him every day.

His father, Clarence, was unable to spend a lot of time with his family in the summer, with the threat of forest fires, he was kept busy with his forestry job.

Duane had a propensity to build things, especially boats. At the age of nine years his parents gave him a cross-cut saw and a square for Christmas. The next Christmas he received a jack plane, and the following year he got a hand brace and bits of three sizes. He still has all these tools today, and they are still in use.

Duane was constantly building shacks and boats. When he was eleven, his father secured enough lumber to build a chicken coop. Enough lumber was snitched from that job to allow Duane to build his first sixteen-foot boat, which was stout enough to run an outboard motor on. Caulking the cracks between planking was done by tapping netting line into them, and painting over it. A good permanent seal.

His cousin, Dallas Gordon, gave him his first outboard which took most of his time to wind and pull to get it started. Trolling Chicago Bay and chumming with Kenneth Koss, across the bay, became Duane's life now. He was on the water and in love with it.

In the early nineteen-forties, deep fishing was starting in Lake Superior, and it was about this time that Duane's uncle, Oscar Sundquist, saw his interest in fishing. Oscar came up with an old sixteen-foot boat and an even older one lung, five-horse-power engine.

Duane Johnson, 1949, and the 1929 Model A.

Duane Johnson with his nineteen-pound, thirty-inch lake trout. Ice fishing, March 29, 2001. Caught in a six-inch hole, taking one hour, forty-six minutes to land. He used an eight-pound test line.

Duane Johnson with another trophy lake trout.

Mounting it as an in-board, it had an iron fly wheel that needed to be cranked to start it. A mile out on the lake, one could hear Duane's boat: *pop, pop, pop,* making its way.

His first momentous fishing experience in the boat was with Kenneth. The lake was calm as glass with them at least two-miles out. Duane hooked a fish that took his breath away. Looking down into the clear water it looked like

59

a whale to him. After a long struggle, he landed the fish, which weighed in at twenty-two pounds. It was this one incident that hooked Duane on deep lake fishing. From that point on he spent hours a day for the rest of the summer catching lake trout. Duane recalls the professional charter fishermen thinking he was nuts for being so far out on the lake at such a young age. From the endless hours he spent on the huge lake, with his friends and alone, he felt he knew what he was doing. Being stranded in the fog, not seeing land for hours, was never a concern to him. He was doing what he loved, and did it well.

When Duane was fourteen, he started building the boat that he would use for commercial fishing, twenty-feet in length. At age sixteen he managed to buy an old Universal in-board for $175. The engine required countless hours putting it together in Uncle Oscar's garage. To take passengers out, the Coast Guard required the operator to have a license, but Duane wasn't old enough. Taking his chances, Duane went into business anyway, and luckily, never came in contact with the Coast Guard. Following the proper order, when Duane turned eighteen he got his license. His income came from charging $2.50 per hour from his customers.

The first year after graduating from high school in 1949, Duane built another boat; this one stretching out to twenty-two feet. His neighbor, Nels Norman, sold Duane an Army Jeep engine which he converted to marine use by adding a water-cooled manifold. At this time he was dating a beautiful young girl named Virginia Schuppel, so it was no coincidence that he named the boat, *Virginia Ann*.

While Duane was still in high school he built a cabin for his mother. Ida Johnson had already had two cabins built, with Duane's becoming the third. Then, after his grandmother, Mary Sundquist Sannes, bought land in Big Bay, he built a cabin for her also. Still a sophomore in high school, he was paid for his work by his grandmother. She gave him 100 feet of land on Big Bay.

Not one to sit idle for any length of time, Duane still found time to help his uncle, Clyde Johnson, on the Moose Valley farm. Putting up hay in the summer, he got his first driving experience hoisting hay up into the barn with the farm truck and pulleys. While his help was definitely needed, and there was no complaint in doing the work, his mind was always on the lake and fishing.

At the age of fifteen he bought his first car, a 1929 Model A, which he used to court his girlfriend, Virginia. One of the fondest memories of that courtship was of the two using the car to go partridge hunting in the fall. The old Ford could take the back trails like no other car could.

Uncle Oscar built a steel boat that he sold to Duane, who was nineteen at the time. Now with two boats for charter fishing, Duane's father would run one of them during busy spells. Finally, at the age of eighteen, Duane got his first fishing license, which led to catching herring with gill nets.

The Susie Islands, out from Grand Portage, became a source of herring for Duane and the friends who helped him. From the middle of October to just before Christmas, salted kegs of herring weighing up to one-hundred pounds each, were put up to keep the catch from spoiling.

For two months they would stay on the island in an old log cabin enjoying the fishing as well as the solitude. One of the interesting features of the island was a copper mine that dated back to the early 1800s era. There was a massive steam boiler on top of a hill which had been picked apart by visitors over time to get the valuable metal from it. Originally weighing many tons, the intriguing boiler was a curiosity. How had it gotten there in the first place? Other than the strange boiler and fishing, their evenings were spent playing whist.

After two months of fishing and playing whist, Duane's real love became most important — Virginia. Duane recalls ordering a Christmas gift for her then, a heart shaped box with mirror, brush, comb. It even played music.

His time divided between boat building, fishing, and courting Virginia, he was a busy young man.

At the end of the fishing season, at the age of nineteen, he went into the pulp business. Working for Consolidated Paper Company 20, north of Hovland, he cut pulp wood with a four-foot hand saw and an axe. With a rented tractor, the logs were skidded out. Even though the work was harder, he made more money logging. The following fall, he went to a dealer in Duluth and bought an Oliver track crawler to do the skidding, aided by a sled he made. Along with his father, the two did all the work by hand. With his business growing, Duane paid $150 for an old Mack truck to move the logs to the landing.

The advent of power saws had Duane buying a McColugh 325 for $350. However, for all the advances in the logging industry, the saw wouldn't start, so he reverted to the old manual logging method until the machine could be fixed. After cutting one tree by hand he decided that he was just too spoiled, and took the McColough to Grand Marais to be repaired.

Duane was a natural when it came to fishing. He understood the moods of the lake and read the weather. Hovland, at one time, was known as the "Lake Trout Capital of the World," drawing many fishermen to the area. When the lamprey infested the lake, the fishing business declined.

The fishing, according to Duane, "Just went to pot," so after logging, his time was spent trapping beaver with his father. The balance of his time was spent entertaining Virginia, stream fishing speckled trout, and swimming in the Brule near the Devil's Kettle, in spite of the mosquitoes.

Concerning the mosquitoes, Virginia recalls, "Duane wore his winter hat with the earlaps down, and I wore a hat with mesh to cover my face. The bugs were terrible, but we had fun."

Chapter 8

Virginia's Maternal Great-Grandparents Mathias and Mari Bergsven (nee Olsdotter Skaars-Eict)

Mathias Bergsven
Born 15 February, 1833 in Lilleulland, Faaberg, Oppland, Norway
Died 4 June, 1917 in Lessor Township, Polk County, Minnesota
Son of Christen Hansen Ulland and Marthe Pedersdotter

Mari Olsdotter Skaars-Eict
Born 14 January, 1832 in Skaars Eict, Ostre Gausdal, Oppland, Norway
Died 23 June, 1920 in Pine Lake Township, Polk County, Minnesota
Daughter of Ole Johansen Skaarslien and Anne Olsdotter

Married: 18 June, 1860 in Ostre Gausdal, Oppland, Norway

Children: Christian Matiasen, b- 8 Mar, 1861
          Ole Matiasen Lilleulland, b- 21 Dec, 1864
          Annetta Matiasdotter, b- 16 Jan, 1869
          Martin Matiasen, b- 17 Nov, 1872

Already married for twenty-three years, Mathias and Mari made the decision to leave their homeland and go to America. On April 14, 1883, they left Lillehammer, Norway, heading for the new land of promises and opportunities to make their dreams come true.

With three children, listed as: Olaf, an infant, Martin, age ten, and Annetta, age fifteen, they drove by sled to Oslo, then by steamship to Liverpool, England. After waiting in Liverpool for one week, they boarded the American Lines steamship, *British Princess*, arriving at the port of Philadelphia on May 10, 1883, almost one month after leaving Ostre Gausdal, Norway. Their oldest son, Christ Matteson at age nineteen, had already gone to America before them in 1880.

At the time of the massive influx of immigrants from Europe, the shipping and customs operations worked on meager resources. At times, information was transcribed with little attention to accuracy. A misspelling of a name or date was taken lightly.

There is an issue of what happened to the second Bergsven son, Ole. One supposition is that he drowned in Norway. Another interesting and unexplained family fact is the presence of the infant named Olaf on the ship's manifest. Thereafter, there is no mention of Ole or Olaf in the collected history of the Bergsven trek. Though Ole is listed as one of the Bergsven children, there is no further history available for either Ole or Olaf in the settlement in America.

The Mathias Bergsven family. Left to right: back row: Martin, Chris, Annette; front row: Mathia and Mari Bergsven.

Almost immediately, Mathias and his family left by train for Zumbrota, Minnesota. One year later, in 1884, the family moved to the Crookston area, homesteading in what was then known as Thirteen Towns. Forty miles from the railroad, the only means of transportation through wild land covered with brush and timber and without roads was by oxen. In recollection, Martin said, "It was kind of hard times, with no work to be had of any kind and no money. But there was plenty of game so we did not starve."

In the summer, they sold snakeroot to be able to buy groceries. Snakeroot pertains to particular plants that were reputed to cure snake bites.

Their first house was made of sod. While warm, it leaked during rainstorms. The flooring was wooden planks cut with a hand saw. In 1887 things got a little easier when the railroad laid tracks and the town of McIntosh, Minnesota, was created. Today, McIntosh, located eighty-two miles northeast of Fargo, in Minnesota, has a population of 610 and remains at least fifty-five percent Norwegian.

Chapter 9

Virginia's Paternal Great-Grandparents Johannes (John) and Mary Schuppel (nee Muscovitz)

Johannes (John) Schuppel
Born 27 January, 1836, in Kircheim, Baden, Germany
Died 27 May, 1920 in Winnona, Minnesota
Son of Friedrich W. Schuppel and Magdalena Kletti

Mary Muskovitz
Born 27 November, 1841, in Erfurt, Germany
Died 31 July, 1917 in Winona, Minnesota
Daughter of John Muscovitz and Mary Fisher

Married 1859 in Milwaukee, Wisconsin

Children: Elizabeth, b- November, 1860

Henry, b- May, 1863	Frederick, b- 4 Sept, 1875
Charles, b- 1863	Susan, b- 4 Sept, 1877
Anna, b- June, 1867	William, b- 4 Oct, 1879
John, b- 3 Oct, 1869	Frank, b- 15 Dec, 1881
Emma, b- 11 Dec, 1871	Edward, b- April, 1884
Otto, b- 2 March, 1873	

Virginia's great-great-grandfather, Friedrich Schuppel gave his family an element of intrigue with his venture to America. In 1852, after having lost two wives, Friedrich Schuppel set out for America from Baden, Germany, with three sons by his second wife, Magdalena. While en route, Friedrich Schuppel died and was buried at sea, leaving the three boys alone on the ship. His death was evidently not sudden, as he had time to make preparations by giving his oldest son, Peter, $100 in gold. Peter, at age eighteen (born in 1834), suddenly had the sole care of his two younger brothers, Johannes (John), born in 1836, and Carl, born in 1843. Arriving in New York, the three orphans were met at the pier by a devious character that spoke German and befriended them. The man invited Peter to have dinner with him, where a dastardly scheme took place.

Peter woke up quite some time later, to find his $100 missing, along with his new friend. As near as Peter could imagine, the man had put "knock out" drops in his drink and robbed him while he was asleep. The three were turned over to a Catholic charity organization that fed and housed the boys. They found work as apprentices at a tobacco packing company. After a spell of stripping tobacco and doing whatever kind of labor they could find, the three moved on to Wisconsin. Peter went to Milwaukee where he would eventually raise a family; with Carl and John moving to Barton, where a half brother lived. Carl, who became known by the name Charles, enlisted in the Union Army to serve in the Civil War for three years. That done, Charles moved to Illinois with a harvesting crew, eventually buying a farm near Springfield. As of 1975, the direct Schuppel descendants were still in possession of the farm.

While in Stoddard, Virginia's grandfather, John, Jr., was born on October 3, 1869, the fifth child of twelve.

Johannes and Mary moved around Wisconsin for a while, eventually leaving Stoddard to end their wanderlust in Winona, Minnesota. Johannes settled down planting his roots in Winona as a shoemaker.

Chapter 10

Virginia's Maternal Grandparents
Martin and Ida Marie Bergsven

Martin Matiasen Bergsven
Born 17 November, 1872 in Vestre Gausdal, Oppland, Norway
Died 20 December, 1956 in Bemidji, Minnesota
Son of Mathias Christensen Bergsven and Mari Olsdotter

Ida Maria Knoll Edwards
Born, 17 February, 1888, in McIntosh, Minnesota.
Died 6 February, 1966 in Bemidji, Minnesota
Daughter of Edward Eriksen Knoll and Lovise Olsdotter

Married 25 June, 1906 in Crookston, Minnesota

Children: Myrtle Elvina, b- 20 Feb, 1907
          Clarence Arthur, b- 11 Feb, 1909
          Leona Marie, b- 27 August, 1912
          Morris Ingvald, b- 29 Jan, 1916
          Marlyce Verna, b- 15 March, 1925

While living in McIntosh, Martin Bergsven met Ida Maria Knoll Edwards. Ida Maria was a beautiful young lady, so when Martin met her, it was inevitable that they would get married. On June 25, 1906, Ida Maria Edwards became Mrs. Martin Bergsven at a ceremony in Crookston, Minnesota. Martin was a mature thirty-four years old, with the lovely Ida was only eighteen.

The couple lived on a farm in McIntosh, Minnesota, for a few years, raising two children there, Myrtle and Clarence.

The details are speculative, but it looks like Martin and his older brother, Christian, went to Montana in 1910, homesteading in an area eighteen miles from Galata, called Grandview, aptly named for the stunning views of Mt. Adams and Mt. Rainier. Today, both Galata and Grandview remain thriving small towns.

Ida Marie Edwards (Bergsven).

Records indicate that Martin built two homes on the homestead, one for himself and one for his parents. This fact alone can indicates that Mathias and Mari were still an integral part of the family. At the time, Mathias was seventy-seven years old, and Mari was seventy-eight.

Later, the remaining family left McIntosh by train, traveling to Galata. Myrtle, Martin's oldest daughter, recalled that they stayed in Galata overnight. This stay would have very likely been the hotel built by David R. McGinnes in 1902. The building, modernized, remains in use today. Galata is famous for their cherry, apple, and pear trees planted by the first settlers and still growing.

Martin and Ida Bergsven, June 25, 1906.

Martin and Ida's daughter Myrtle recollected, "The next day we traveled eighteen miles in a wagon pulled by horses. We also had two oxen named 'Buck' and 'Pete.'"

Recalling the desolate prairie they lived on, Myrtle also said, "Wood was very hard to come by. We would have to go out and pick up buffalo chips for fires. My mother thought it was terrible that we had to bake bread and use buffalo chips as fuel." Myrtle's memory was dim about the length of time they spent in Grandview, but she was certain it was at least one winter.

Life in Montana was every bit as difficult as it was in Minnesota, with work for pay being extremely hard to find. Fortunately, Martin got a job running the local post office.

On the farm in McIntosh. Left to right: Martin, Ida, Mari, Myrtle, and Clarence.

Martin and Ida Bergsven, 1944.

On August 27, 1912, Virginia's mother, Leona Marie, was born upstairs in the Bergsven home, the only child born in Montana.

Possibly due to homesickness, the family was prompted to move back to McIntosh soon after Leona's birth. While back in McIntosh, Morris Ingvald was born, on January 29, 1916.

Wanderlust was certainly bred into the Martin Bergsven family. In 1917, they sold their farm in

Martin and Ida Bergsven, August 2, 1953.

McIntosh, and the whole family went back to Kalispell, Montana, but only for a period of six months. Myrtle recalled her mother, Ida's, discomfort with the altitude. She was sick much of the time. So, now being seasoned travelers, they moved back to McIntosh where Martin worked in a grocery store.

The last move by the Bergsvens came three years later, in 1920, when they trekked to Bemidji, Minnesota. Martin found employment on the railroad and also worked in a store part time. The Bergsven family felt they had finally settled where they belonged, and Bemidji, Minnesota was their last stop.

On March 15, 1925, the youngest daughter, Marlyce, was born.

Chapter 11

Virginia's Paternal Grandparents
John and Minnie Schuppel

John Schuppel
Born 3 October, 1869 in Stoddard, Wisconsin
Died 3 September, 1937 in Winona, Minnesota
Son of Johannes Schuppel and Marry Muskovitz

Louise Wilhelmine (Minnie) Caroline Hahn
Born 23 February, 1874 in Fountain City, Wisconsin
Died 6 September, 1951 in Warroad, Minnesota
Daughter of Casper Friedrich Georg Hahn and Maria
Wilhelmine Elisabeth Langfeldt

Married 23 June, 1897 in Winona, Minnesota

Children: Arthur Schuppel, b- 25 Dec, 1900
Harold Louis Willard, b- 30 August, 1902

John Schuppel, Jr., Virginia's grandfather, was a tall slender young man with dark-brown eyes and a mane of dark-brown hair. A darker complexion was a typical Schuppel trait that can

The John Schuppel family, about 1908.
Left to right: John, Art, Minnie, and Harold.

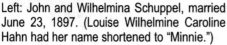

Left: John and Wilhelmina Schuppel, married
June 23, 1897. (Louise Wilhelmine Caroline
Hahn had her name shortened to "Minnie.")

also be seen in Virginia. John worked primarily as a painter. He was
the fifth child of a family of twelve.

While in Winona, John, Jr., met and married Wilhelmine Hahn,
known as Minnie, on June 23, 1897. A tall large-boned girl of heavy
German heritage, Minnie had blonde hair and blue eyes. She was
born in Fountain City, Wisconsin, on February 23, 1874. Her father,
also a shoemaker, came to America from Holstein, Germany, with his
wife, Maria, and settled in Winona. Minnie's father, Casper, died
September 6, 1908, of cancer.

John and Minnie's wedding took place June 23, 1897, in Winona.
John and Minnie had two boys; Arthur and Harold Louis Willard,
who would eventually become Virginia's father.

Chapter 12

Virginia's Parents
Harold Louis Willard and Leona Marie Schuppel

Harold Louis Willard Schuppel
Born 30 August, 1902 in Winona, Minnesota
Died 28 December, 1964 in Hovland, Minnesota
Son of John Schuppel and Louise Wilhelmine (Minnie) Caroline
Hahn

Leona Marie Bergsven
Born 27 August, 1912 in Grandview, Montana
Died 14 September, 1981 in Grand Marais, Minnesota
Daughter of Martin Bergsven and Ida Marie Knoll Edwards

Married 20 June, 1931 in Bemidji, Minnesota

Children: Virginia Ann, b- 9 May, 1932
John Harold, b- 21 January, 1934

Harold Louis Willard Schuppel

HAROLD GREW UP IN WINONA. After graduating from high school, he attended and graduated from Dunwoody Institute in Minneapolis. In April 1923, Harold began his lifelong career in forestry, starting as a draftsman in the St. Paul Forestry office, located in the old capitol building. In due time, Harold became a lookout tower builder, with complete charge of

Harold Schuppel, April 5, 1931.

John Schuppel family, 1931. Left to right: Art, Minnie, John, and Harold.

tower construction. His complex duties included laying out the base plans, setting tower piers, doing the steel work, checking the completed structure, and supervising the erection crews.

In doing his job, Harold met a pretty young girl, Leona Marie Bergsven, a stenographer at the Bemidji and St. Paul offices. The wedding took place on June 20, 1931, in Bemidji, Minnesota.

The Forestry Service transferred Harold to Grand Rapids, Minnesota, where he assumed the job of forest ranger. In the early

thirties, the family was indeed for-
tunate to have housing provided by
the Forestry Service. It was in
Grand Rapids that the Schuppel
side of the Johnson saga began with
the birth of their first child, Virginia
Ann, on May 9, 1932. Her brother,
John Harold, was born January 21,
1934.

Harold and Leona Schuppel, August 19,
1959.

Chapter 13

Virginia Ann Schuppel

arold Louis Willard Schuppel and his wife, Leona Marie, moved to Grand Rapids, Minnesota. Harold was a forest ranger with the benefit of a house provided by the Forestry Department. In the hard-pressed days of the early 1930s, the home, large yard, and abundance of surrounding pine trees was welcome, indeed.

On the pleasant day of May 9, 1932, in the town of Grand Rapids, Minnesota, Virginia Ann Schuppel was introduced to the world at 5:30 a.m. at the Itasca Hospital. Two years later, brother John Harold Schuppel was born on January 21, 1934.

Normal healthy and energetic children, Virginia and her brother spent their time playing in their big sand pile, swimming in Lake Pokegama, fishing, and walking along the beach. Virginia recalls the lush carpet of white trilliums that covered the yard. They had mallard ducks as pets, "It was always fun to watch the babies. We also had chickens, so we always had fresh eggs. In the winter we went sliding on the hills and had ponds we could skate on."

Virginia belonged to the Brownies, Girl Scouts, and was active in the youth choir at church. She remembers it was a big choir with a good leader to keep it together. Besides the singing, she took part in a lot of activities. Virginia's participation in her church was something she carried with her through her life.

Virginia Schuppel and John Koss with a twenty-five-pound lake trout caught by Virginia in 1948.

On December 26, 1945, Virginia's family moved from Grand Rapids to Hovland, where Harold became forestry supervisor. Settling his family into a small house beside the Flute Reed River, Harold had charge of several men who did road work, cruised timber, and fought forest fires. Later, the Forestry Department sold the land their house was on, moving its headquarters to Grand Marais. The house was later sold and moved about three blocks, where Tim and Jan Hall refurbished it, and where Jan still lives today.

Virginia started school in Grand Marais in the eighth grade, and then graduated in 1950. The one-room school was a disappointment after the advanced system she attended in Grand Rapids. Her brother, Jack, was in the sixth grade then, so attended class in the Chicago Bay School where there were six combined grades with just one teacher.

Skating on the clear ice of Lake Superior, she could look to the bottom and the rocks laying there. This clear lake ice was cut into blocks in the winter and covered with sawdust to keep food cold year around. There are those who believe only this ice can make the world's best ice cream.

The town hall, located next to the Forestry building, was where family events and dances took place. According to Virginia, there always seemed to be an accordion in the bands that played there. Music was an appreciation that followed Virginia, whether it was singing, or playing.

Hovland boasted two stores at the time, and Duane's Aunt Millie Mainella and Uncle Charlie had one, which also held the post office, and Aunt Millie was the postmistress. The store seemed to have just about everything a person would want—groceries, hardware, fishing supplies, and even plumbing parts. Virginia's mother, Leona Marie, did substitute work in the post office, becoming the postmistress when Aunt Millie retired.

At the time of this writing, Millie Mainella is alive and well, celebrating 101 years of life. Millie enjoys painting, walking, and loves to read. Duane and Virginia's daughter, Dusty, is a frequent visitor with Millie and was a major contributor of family history to make this book possible.

When Virginia turned fifteen, the inevitable happened, and she started dating Duane. Sporting his Model A Ford coupe, Duane was quite the dashing figure. Virginia shared a comment that, "That old coupe was pretty neat." With a shared fondness for the outdoors, Duane and Virginia went fishing and hunting whenever they could. Stream fishing for speckled trout was fun, but the bugs were a constant nuisance. A favorite spot was in Portage Brook, until the DNR had to poison out Devilfish Lake. Portage Brook was an outflow from the lake, so fishing there was halted.

When Virginia was fourteen, she started working at the Mainella store during the summers. She pumped gasoline, checked oil and washed windows, along with working the check-out counter inside. Virginia and her mom and dad went deep-lake fishing in Lake Superior, often with John Koss. Among the many memorable events of her youth, one that stands out is when Virginia caught a twenty-five pound lake trout on one of these fishing trips.

A favorite memory for Virginia is the week during the summer when she visited Grandma and Grandpa Bergsven on their farm in Bemidji. Can you imagine anything better than a big bowl of fresh picked strawberries covered with their own cream, straight from the cow? Grandpa Bergsven was a State Fair prize winner many times over for his strawberries. Grandpa's rhubarb stood taller than Virginia. The old Model A coupe was special, with a rumble seat for Virginia and her brother, Jack.

The tradition for Thanksgiving was a trip to the farm, where Grandma Ida fixed a huge turkey and, of course, lefsa, and glorified rice. The house filled with family, the business of the day, and all being together is a memory Virginia holds close.

The mouth of Brule River was the best swimming for them then. Up from the highway and below the Devils Kettle was the warmest spot. Virginia said, "The current was pretty strong there, but we still enjoyed it." Now, the Devils Kettle is a part of the Judge C. R. Magney State Park. Any visitor to the park can stand on the footbridge over the Brule and watch in wonder at where the water goes as it swirls down into the kettle.

When Virginia graduated from Cook County High School, in 1950, she left the very next day for Minneapolis to attend The Minnesota School of Business. Graduating in February, 1951, she expressed interest in working for the FBI, and put in her application. The president of her school arranged an interview with an FBI agent in Minneapolis, which took place on the same day her parents went to the Cities to pick her up.

Not too long ago, my wife and I were sitting in Duane and Virginia's home sharing a cup of coffee. Looking out the living room windows at the vastness of Lake Superior, the conversation led to the time when Virginia left for Washington. After all the time that had passed, I could still sense the foreboding feeling that Duane must have felt when she left. He commented, "I thought she was gone. I didn't think I'd ever see her again."

After an investigation into her background, Virginia was offered a job in Washington, D.C. The FBI housed her in a motel while they processed her. She met a girl from South Dakota who became her roommate. The FBI found a house for them located across the street from a large park, which made the stay away from home more enjoyable. She thoroughly enjoyed her work at the Justice Department, commuting by bus, and Virginia is proud to state that, at the time, her boss was J. Edgar Hoover.

She took in the sights and interesting tours around D.C., but didn't get to see the inside of the White House, as they were renovating it. This is the time when President Harry Truman and his family were living in the Blair House.

Virginia doesn't comment too much on her work for the FBI, other than saying, "I got to see information on many things before anybody else in the country did. I had an FBI escort every time I left the building."

Virginia's grandmother, Wilhemenia, was ill, so she flew home to see her. She died a few days later, with the funeral held in Winona. At the time, Virginia was involved in the wedding of Larry and Dorothy Peterson, in Hovland. This was a special occasion as this was just the third wedding to be performed in the new Trinity Church.

While she was home in Hovland, just after the wedding, Duane asked Virginia to marry him, with a resounding answer of yes. Much to Duane's disappointment, Virginia had to fly back to Washington, D.C., and work until the end of the year. At the next Christmas, Virginia returned to Hovland, where, just after the holiday, Duane presented her with a diamond engagement ring.

Chapter 14

Duane and Virginia Johnson

Clarence Duane Johnson
Born, 16 June, 1931 in Duluth, Minnesota
Son of Clarence August and Ida Josephine Johnson

Virginia Ann Schuppel
Born, 9 May, 1932 in Grand Rapids, Minnesota
Daughter of Harold Louis Willard and Leona Marie Schuppel

Children: Sandra Jean, b- 14 November, 1952
Rocky Duane, b- 25 January, 1955
Dusty Lynn, b- 2 November, 1958
Stoney Lance, b- 10 October, 1960
Rusty Scott, b- 20 March, 1962
Misty Dawn, b- 17 July, 1964

On Valentines Day, February 14, 1952, Duane and Virginia were married at the Trinity Lutheran Church of Hovland, presided by the Pastor, Rolf G. Hanson. A quiet simple ceremony, her brother Jack was the best man, with Marie Norman as her bride's maid. Charlie Mainella rented a small but cozy cabin to the new Johnson's, located near the store. The spring of 1952 came early, so Duane set out to build a cabin on the land he got from his grandmother, on Big Bay.

The ever ambitious Johnson's decided to build a motel. It seemed like a good idea as Duane's mother, Ida, had been doing very well renting cabins to tourists, taking advantage of the excellent Lake Superior fishing. The land was purchased from Duane's Aunt Helen, and along with his grandmother's cabin to rent out, they were in the tourist business also. Starting in 1957, with an Oliver crawler tractor, Duane dug gravel from the beach to mix with cement for the foundation. Taking his spare time to do the building, it was almost two years in the making. With a bank loan to finish it, the Johnsons did everything except the wiring.

Duane and Virginia Johnson, married February 14, 1952, in Trinity Lutheran Church, Hovland, Minnesota.

Over a period of about eighteen years, the Buck-Doe Motel brought many interesting people into their lives, but after so long, it just became too much. The Buck-Doe Motel was sold to Larry Ryden, who moved it further north to become a part of the Ryden Border Store. As the last stop for anyone leaving the United States, or the first sight for anyone leaving Canada, the Ryden Border Store still operates the motel.

With three children, Sandy, Rocky, and Dusty, the cabin the Johnsons lived in was getting cramped. One bedroom, a tiny living room, and a small kitchen—this small space was overrun with family, the laundry, and supplies for the motel.

Duane and Virginia's cabin, March 1, 1952.

There was no question about it, they needed a bigger house. After being vacated, the tiny cabin was far from being vacant, though. Over a period of time, it was lived in by Virginia's brother, Jack; Duane's sister Arline; Duane's father, Clarence; Dusty and Eric; and Aunt Millie. Then, Rusty moved the cabin across Highway 61 to his property, dug and poured a foundation, and set the cabin onto its current site. Now the home of Bob and Jeanine Swearingen, the small cabin has been shelter to a lot of people, all in the Johnson clan.

At the time they were building the motel, Duane became more involved in logging. After a forest fire north of Tom Lake, Duane got a bargain price on some large standing pine stumpage. Hauling the timber to Bill Deater's sawmill, they were cut into thick and thin planks, then stacked to dry for a year. After, it was hauled to Hedstrom's mill, in Grand Marais, to be planed. Later, Duane bought a sawmill from Otis Anderson. With Rusty using it first to build his own house, Duane and Rusty worked together, as it took two to run the saw, feed in the timber, and pull out the lumber. Cutting thick and thin planks with any precision takes a great deal of practice and skill.

To build their new house, Duane bought white pine at a sale, and then ran it through his mill. He hired Clyde Wishcop to do the stone work, but tragedy took over, and Clyde was killed in an automobile accident. Clyde had been a fast worker, with the slower moving Duane learning the craft as he helped. The floor plan was designed by Virginia, with the construction being Duane's job, as it just came to him naturally.

With a gift for building, Duane constructed a cabin every year, for about ten years. Houses from Duane's labor were put up for Ben Gessner, in Big Bay; Les Gould and Jack Schneider, east of Big Bay. Duane did construction out at Tom Lake for Dale Hooper, and Lloyd Irish, also. Then, he built a more complicated home for Jerry Steinwall at Tom Lake, as well as a small cabin near the Naniboujou Lodge on Lake Superior. Later, Duane helped Rocky build his home, then one similar to it for his sister Arline.

The Buckdoe Motel on Highway 61, Hovland, Minnesota, September 1956.

Duane's friend of fifty years, Cliff Cowherd, had a Johnson-built cabin set on a hill overlooking McFarland Lake. Duane and Cliff went on many portages to East Pike, and MacFarland from the Gunflint Trail.

Cliff passed away recently, and Duane recalls some of the wonderful times they had canoeing the Boundary Waters Canoe Area (BWCA). Starting at Gunflint Lake, they paddled a couple days to reach Mountain Lake, which was known for trout fishing. They had lunch on an island in Mountain Lake, on the Canadian side. Cliff called it, "The Queen's Island." Mountain Lake was a good ten miles long, and after leaving the island around noon, they paddled almost to the end, when Duane asked Cliff for one of the candy bars they had as a provision. However, to get the candy bars, they had to paddle back to the island where they had left them. By the time they reached the end of the lake, it was getting dark. This was obviously a good time to go fishing. After pulling in a few trout, it was so dark they

Home of Duane and Virginia Johnson in Big Bay, Hovland, Minnesota, November 1, 2005.

could barely tell where the shoreline was. Duane recalled, "It was the darkest dark I've ever seen."

The next day they moved on to Moose Lake and got a little more fishing in before setting up the tent for the night. After a full night of rain that dragged into the next day, the trip to the end of Moose Lake netted them a canoe so full of water they had trouble keeping it upright. The voyage went to North Fowl Lake, up the Royal River, to Big John Lake, and to Little John Lake, finally back to McFarland.

Many of us have taken trips like Duane and Cliff did, and they remain as some of the memories we like to pull out from time to time. Friends pass on, but the memories stay behind to keep them close to us.

The Johnsons bought a piece of land on Tom Lake, where Duane altered his customary cabin design. He built a pontoon using four aircraft pontoons. At first, they would anchor in the lake, midway between their property and an island. With the three small kids in tow, they lived on the lake, with fishing and swimming right outside the door.

One eventful morning, to take the chill out of the air, a kettle of water was put on to boil in the boats galley. However, even with the precaution of leaving a window open, they suffered from near asphyxiation.

Today, the pontoon boat is pulled ashore, serving mostly as a changing place, or a quick shelter from the weather. The Tom Lake spot is a paradise, with a sandy beach, a ramp for launching boats, and a wonderful picnic area. Many family and friends have spent wonderful times not only enjoying the recreation offered at the spot, but also the hospitality of these gracious people.

Besides the love of fishing, there are a few other things the Johnsons love. One of them being anything with an internal combustion engine mounted on it. Virginia had a deep love for motorcycles, but as soon as the boys were able to swing a leg over the seat, she was left behind. The fever didn't escape Dusty either, who just recently got one for herself. No matter the season or the reason, there is going to be a Johnson with their legs wrapped around an engine.

Pets were just as prevalent as motors. A couple of cockers named Pebbles and Rebel, a poodle called Frostee, and a black woodchuck who had the run of the house, trained to used a litter pan. What kid wouldn't want a woodchuck hogging the pillow all night? He was a part of the Johnson family for about five years and had a fondness for doughnuts. On that diet, he grew to fifteen pounds. He was a favorite at school for show and tell. Then there was the snapping turtle that was one inch in diameter when Sandy got it. When it grew to a foot in diameter, it was time to release it into Stump River.

One other thing the Johnson's have is an appetite. A favorite among the kids was *Kropkakor*, made with potatoes and salt pork. As a new bride, Duane's mother prompted Virginia to learn how to make it, with the kids always watchful that nobody got more than their fair share. At one time, Virginia had to roll out one-hundred-eighty of them.

Duane grew up on a Christmas tradition of *lutefisk*, but after a couple of years, she put her foot down, "That was it!"

The influence the Johnsons have had on the community is reflected by their offspring. From the beginning of the influx to America, every member of the family, on all sides, has lived with an ethic of doing a good job in an honest manner. There is hardly a person in Cook County that cannot look with admiration to someone they know in the Johnson family.

The first child, Sandra Jean (Sandy) was born November 14, 1952, in Duluth. Being the only grandchild to either of the extended families, the little girl was the center of attention. After graduating from high school, Sandy worked at the Hovland Forestry tower, before she married her first husband, Orvis, who also worked for the Forestry. By that time, Virginia's mother, Leona, was the postmistress, Sandy did substitute work. At this writing, Sandy is the postmistress, just a short time from retirement. Sandy and her husband, Bruce Updyke, built a log home in Moose Valley, where Sandy runs a photography studio.

Duane and Virginia's second child, a son they named Rocky Duane, was born January 25, 1955. Fishing just seemed to run like blood in the Johnson family. At age ten, Rocky caught his first two steelhead trout out from the Reservation River, in Lake Superior. He pulled the fish in like a pro, but it was just as exciting for his parents.

After high school, Rocky took up trucking and was in a serious accident in Two Harbors that almost took his life. A thirty-foot-high pile of pulp logs rolled on him, pinning him to the side of his truck, completely burying him. After digging him out, he went by helicopter to a Duluth hospital. Recovering, Rocky invoked his Johnson fortitude and is still hauling pulp today. Anytime harm comes to a child, it is devastating to a family. On this occasion, the accident happened just one day before Duane and Virginia were to celebrate their fiftieth wedding anniversary.

On February 11, 1958, Duane and Virginia's third child and second daughter, Dusty Lynn, was born in Duluth. After graduating from school in Grand Marais, she worked at the Johnson (no relation) Grocery store there. Being a tireless worker, she also spent time with her dad in the woods helping him. She eventually got a job in the courthouse in Grand Marais, where she has impressive responsibility for Cook County. Dusty married Eric Nelms, who worked for the State Fishery Department.

Stoney Lance was born October 10, 1960, in St. Lukes Hospital, in Duluth. Virginia remembered that it was on a Monday and she was in labor until 10:25 p.m. Starting kindergarten in 1966, he graduated from Cook County High School in 1979. A proud point his mother makes is that Stoney had perfect attendance all through school. Virginia says, "Stoney was a typical boy and had to learn things the hard way." He loved to fish and hunt partridge. His mom told of one of his more memorable moments, "Stoney was partridge hunting on his bike and piled up, bending the barrel of his .410 like a bow."

Stoney then went to East Grand Forks to learn truck driving. He stayed at the fire hall, going out on fire calls to pay for his rent while he was there. Back in Grand Marais, he worked for Edwin Thoreson doing road construction for several years. Quitting Thoreson's, he tried working in Texas for a couple of years in the winter. However, with poor pay and a humid environment, he returned home to Grand Marais. Stoney bought land and a home about six miles up the Gunflint Trail. Having not found the right woman yet, he remains single. Still driving truck, Stoney says he has more time for fishing now than he has had in years. In an article for Art Lundquist's eighty-fifth birthday, Stoney said about his motorcycling, "I made it all the way to the second round eliminations at Brainerd International Raceway with a 100 miles per hour, 13.9 second, one mile run on my Kawasaki. I've gone faster and quicker, but local law enforcement could never catch me to verify it."

Rusty Scott was born March 20, 1962, at St. Lukes, in Duluth. Graduating from Cook County High School on May 30, 1980, he went on to Duluth Vo-Tech to learn auto and diesel mechanics. Rusty was a mechanic at the Cobblestone Dealership in Grand Marais until they sold the business. Choosing not to stay with the new owners, Rusty took a job with the County Highway Department, stationed in Hovland, where he happily works close to home.

Misty Dawn was born July 17, 1964, also at St. Lukes Hospital in Duluth. Virginia recalls the record heat wave then, topping off at ninety-four degrees. Following the flow of her brothers and sisters, she graduated from Cook County High School on June 4, 1982. In September of that year she went to Duluth Vo-Tech where she met a classmate of Rusty's, Tim Schliep. She worked briefly at the Cobblestone Dealership, she left to marry Tim on September 15, 1984, at the Trinity Lutheran Church in Hovland. Tim's mother and dad, Jim and Mary Schliep, and Ozzie Peterson, played at the dance in the Hovland Town Hall.

A few days later, Tim and Misty left for Alaska, but the distance from family was too hard to handle, so after ten years they moved back, building a home in Schroeder.

Chapter 15

Trinity Lutheran Church
Hovland, Minnesota

There is one outstanding quality about the Johnson family obvious to anyone. Every member of the family is brought up with an ethic that hard honest work is the only way to get from morning to evening, or from birth to death, in a condition to make them proud.

From the beginning, Duane Johnson would put his entire effort into doing the very best he could, no matter what it was. Building boats, logging, doing work for others, or raising a family, it didn't matter what the job was, he did it with honor. Work your butt off all week, but on Sunday, things changed.

Sunday was family day, starting with church. Then it was into the car for a trip, a picnic, or more often, some fishing. Going to church was the pivot point that everything centered around, and the little church in Hovland became a part of their lives.

The following is taken from the Centennial Anniversary Celebration of Trinity Lutheran Church, Hovland, Minnesota, September 12, 1909 to August 29, 2009.

The Early Years
An excerpt contributed by Elsie Palmer.

Early in the month of July 1905, a courageous and dedicated young man left his home in Pennsylvania and traveled to Grand Marais to begin his work in the Lutheran Church there and to assist Reverend Stacy in his ministry to the pioneer settlers along the North Shore of Lake Superior. During the following seventeen months, the young man, Reverend Gable, conducted worship services all the way from Beaver Bay to Hovland, a formidable task because of the hardships in travel in those days. The record shows that during this time Reverend Gable traveled a total of 3,904 miles: 1,058 miles on foot, 2,532 by boat, and 314 on the stage.

In the pioneer settlement of Hovland at that time, there were no religious services, no church building, and no organized congregation. The settlers were dependent upon itinerant ministers who occasionally

The first Trinity Lutheran Church.

visited Hovland. With the arrival of Reverend Gable in Grand Marais, the people of Hovland were able to have services more often.

The first of these services was held September 9, 1905, on a Thursday evening. Reverend Gable walked all the way to Hovland, returning to Grand Marais on the steamer *America* that same night. From then on he held services at Hovland about once a month until November 1906, when he left to take charge of a Lutheran mission in Superior, Wisconsin.

Early in the summer of 1907, Reverend Carl Eidnes, who had just been ordained, was called to take charge of the Norwegian Lutheran Church in Grand Marais.

At a meeting of interested residents of Hovland on August 10, 1907, a Norwegian Lutheran congregation was organized and called the Zion Congregation. The officers elected were: Reverend Eidnes, chairman; Louis Ellingsen, secretary; Martin Jacobsen, treasurer; John Eliasen, Louis Ellingsen, and John Jacobsen, trustees; Hjalmer Eliasen, janitor; Mattie Jacobsen, organist; John Jacobsen, usher.

From then on services were held in Hovland on the average of once every three weeks, usually in the Chicago Bay School. The minister made the trip from Grand Marais by horse and sleigh in winter and by horse and buggy when the ground was bare. It was necessary for him to stay overnight at Ellingsen's Hotel, returning to Grand Marais the next day.

In 1906 more settlers arrived, taking up homesteads farther inland, where they hoped to farm. One settlement was known as Poplar Hill; another one, also an inland community, was called Flutereed Valley. Both new settlements were located about four miles from Chicago Bay, a considerable distance in those days of almost impassable roads. A September 1907 issue of the *Cook County News Herald* said, "More and better roads is the crying need of Hovland Township."

The formation of a second congregation was necessitated by the travel difficulties in going to Chicago Bay. Trinity Lutheran was organized on September 12, 1909. On January 17, 1910, the annual pay for Reverend Eidnes was set at $75.00.

On August 1, 1912, the Zion congregation was dissolved and joined with Trinity.

On March 17, 1913, at a meeting in the Flutereed School, it was decided that the community would build a church of their own. Professor R.M. Hall and his father were paid $500 to do the construction. The finished building was an impressive figure, twenty-eight by forty feet, with a nineteen-foot ceiling, and reaching fifty-seven feet to the top of the steeple. It had a capacity to hold 250 people. The first service was held October 12, 1913. The first seating was provided by planks on nail kegs. Plans were made to buy five dozen chairs, which were used up until the construction of the next new church in 1948.

The sermons were spoken in Norwegian. The women and children sat on the west side, and the men sat on the east side. At the meeting of May 1926, women were granted permission to vote at annual meetings.

By 1937 it was recognized that church attendance was declining. A decision was made to move the building to a site somewhere on the new Highway 61. The need for a more convenient location was hampered by the Great Depression looming over their finances. The total income for the church in 1936 was $280.91. In January 1944, the decision was made to tear down the old church, use as much of the material as possible, the most prominent being the main doors, and the wooden floor, and build a new building.

On February 8, 1946, a lot slightly larger than two acres on Highway 61, was purchased from the State of Minnesota for $219.70.

According to the historical records in the *One Hundred Year Commemoration* book, it was on July 2, 1947 when the foundation for the new church was poured.

To help with the construction, a group of students from St. Olaf College came up for the summer and started a work camp. They stayed at Mons Hanson's farm. Virginia kept a record of them: Alice Erlander,

Beresford, South Dakota; Erma Gangsel, Northfield, Minnesota; Faythe Nelson, Arlington, South Dakota; Edwin Barsness, Black Earth, Wisconsin; William Dion, Minneapolis, Minnesota; William Ostroot, Little Falls, Minnesota; and Marilyn Morgenson, Rochester, Minnesota. With Arnold Flatten in charge of the group, the locals and the students seemed to get along very well. Harold Schuppel, Virginia's dad, spent all the spare time he could on the construction. Having to hold services in the Chicago Bay school house, where Virginia played the piano, put a special emphasis on the project. She also helped teach Sunday school, which was natural, as the whole family was involved with the church.

Mons Hanson was typical of the hard working pioneers that helped develop Hovland. He was born in Norway, on December 27, 1877, coming to Hovland in 1909. He trapped in Cook County for forty years. One day he was in the woods checking his trap line when he suffered a broken hip. He spent forty-two hours in the woods, and it took two hours to carry him to his old homestead. He was taken to Duluth in an ambulance, but died from the injury. His funeral was held in the new Trinity Church, and he is buried in the Hovland cemetery. An interesting note is that Mons Hanson and his wife were at the dedication of the new church, and he helped build the first church, as well. His home was located on a farm near the Brule River, about seven miles from the church.

The building committee consisted of Harold Schuppel, chairman, Anton Arnquist, Gordon Finley, Arthur Ongstad, Carl Thorson, and Nels Norman, church treasurer. The church was designed by Professor Arnold Flaten, of St. Olaf College, in Northfield.

Another group of volunteers arrived June 23: Armand Asper, Canton, South Dakota; Oliver Carlson, Northfield, Minnesota; Ruth Johnson, Fargo, North Dakota; and Les Larson, Superior, Wisconsin. In addition, Professor Harold Ditmanson and his wife came to spend a week.

The entire group was given living quarters at the Mons Hansen and the Georgia Flynn homes. The Flynn property had been purchased by Professor Howard Hong. The group was transported to the work site on a trailer furnished by Oscar Sundquist, and pulled by a Jeep loaned to the camp. Interestingly, the Jeep was driven by Hong in Germany in 1945 and 1946. Anton Arnquist loaned the group his cow, providing fresh milk and cream. Fishermen along the shore stopped by to donate part of their catch to be sure they all had enough to eat.

The first service in the Trinity Lutheran Church was held Sunday night, January 18, 1948, in the basement, with Reverend Edmonds officiating. Reverend Edmonds was also minister in Grand Marais, where he lived, as well as Tofte and Lutsen.

Everybody in the community came together, whether they were a congregation member, or not. Harold Schuppel and Clarence Johnson worked together doing whatever needed to be done. Virginia proudly talks about the special jobs that her dad, Harold, did.

"He put the stained-glass window together, built many of the pews, made the altar and lectern, and the communion rail." Marie Lindemann and Marge Fay made the altar garments and the stoles. Dorothy (Koss) Peterson was the musician at the time, with Virginia as the assistant, on an old pump organ in the basement. Virginia is still playing the organ.

As hard as the St. Olaf volunteers worked, they were treated to a good time. Local fishermen took them deep lake fishing, and there were many beach parties.

During the summer of 1948, another group of volunteers arrived from St. Olaf. Robert Bergesen, Chicago; Anne Harang, Belview, Minnesota; and Beatrice Helgen, Northfield, Minnesota. Bill Smith attended Carlton College and was a star as their foremost wrestler. Also, Ivan Fagre, Norris Erdal, and Morris Schmidt were volunteers, but their home towns are unknown.

Dedication for the church took place July 16, 1950, with over two-hundred people attending. The address was given by Dr. P.S. Dybvig, director of Home Missions, ELC.

The church had a Conn organ installed on April 24, 1958, and was replaced by an Allen organ, dedicated July 18, 1982, purchased from Schmitt Music in Rosedale, for $5,995.00.

From 1907 to 1945, a variety of ministers held service in Hovland: C.G. Eidnes, 1907 to 1912; Thomas G. Sandeno, 1912 to 1916; H.F. Johnson, 1917 to 1921; H.M. Herstad, 1922 to 1929; P. Lauritz Mork, 1030 to 1932; James O. Peterson, 1932 to 1938; Jerrold L. Moilien, 1939 to 1945. Most came by horse and buggy, with Pastor Sandeno building a small stable at the church for the benefit of his horse.

The first minister of the new church was Aubrey L. Edmonds, 1946 to 1950. He also pitched in and spent many hours laboring with the rest of the volunteers. After Rev. Edmonds came; Rolf G. Hanson, 1951 to 1954; Steward D. Govig, 1954 to 1957; Joel Anderson, 1958 to 1966; Joseph P. Nystuen, 1966 to 1970; Robert H. Stoskopf, 1970 to 1988; and Mark Osthus, 1988 to 1993. There was short stint by Pastor Edmund until 1994, being replaced by John Hogenson-Rutford, who was regarded as an exceptional minister, leaving in 2006.

Trinity Lutheran Church, Hovland, Minnesota.

The current minister, Kristin Valborg Rolvaag Garey, was installed as an intern on December 2, 2006. At a very impressive ordination service on April 19, 2008, when Pastor Garey became the Trinity Lutheran minister. This was the first time the Hovland church had its own. In October 2003, the congregation agreed to buy the Holland house which stood next door to the parish, creating the first parsonage, where Reverend Kristin and her husband, Mike, live.

History of the church shows that as early as 1905, when there was no church building, Reverend Gable walked twenty miles from Grand Marais to Hovland to hold services once a month. In the evening he would take the steamer, *America*, back to Grand Marais. An interesting note here is that to commemorate the one-hundredth anniversary of the church, Reverend Garey recreated Reverend Gables trek by walking from Grand Marais to Hovland.

One of the reasons this little church has remained so special to the people of Hovland is the love and unselfish giving that went into its construction. It stands as more than a place to worship; it is where friends and neighbors meet to hold hands, sing, pray, and just plain chitchat. It's what people in a small community do.

Chapter 16

Fishing and Hunting

I f there was a force behind the Johnson family that guided their life, aside from the church, it would be fishing and hunting. Inside Rusty and Kathi's house guns are mounted to the wall, as well as moose head trophies, and fishing gear is usually piled up in the corner. Kathi is constantly picking up after her four men, but where life keeps moving. During a recent phone conversation with Kathi, her discourse was constantly interrupted with bellows away from the phone, "Get away from my cookie batter." However, one mention of a jaunt to Tom Lake, and the family is in focus and all the trappings magically appear with the boat hooked up to the truck.

At the coming of deer season an anticipated phone call from Paul and Theresa, in Buffalo, starts the preparation. "We're on the way." No matter who gets the first lucky shot out in the woods, the real drive behind the hunt is that the family is together. With over 170 acres of pristine wilderness, the Johnsons are in tune with what they have, and become a part of it.

With her incredible mind working its way into the past, Virginia drew out some early nostalgia of one of her and Duane's favorite pastimes, fishing. In her own words; "The first time we ever went fishing through the ice, we went to Devilfish Lake. At the time, there were a lot of lake trout there. It was a cold and windy day, and we weren't getting any bites. Some friends were fishing in a different spot on the lake, and they had their limits and were on the way out. They told us to go ahead and use their holes, and we caught our limit, just like that. We were sold on winter fishing after that, and still enjoy it."

One of Duane and Virginia's favorite lakes for winter fishing was Mountain Lake. At one time they had to navigate several portages to get there, but since access to the lake is restricted by the BWCA, the portages are no longer accessible.

Virginia tells of one outstanding trip to Mountain Lake, "Duane got a big fish on, but only had a six inch hole. We had to cut them by hand then. I went over to his hole in case I had to help him, but it took one hour and forty-five minutes to get the fish in. In the meantime, I went back to my hole and caught a couple trout. He had an eight pound test line so really had to be careful. I had a stronger line on my pole, so when he finally got the head started in the hole, I dropped my line down and got a hook in the fish's mouth. We both pulled but couldn't get the fish up. I finally reached down into the mouth with my hand and pulled it up. It weighed nineteen pounds and was thirty-eight inches long—a nice lake trout."

When their kids were little, they were taken to Mountain Lake where fish were always caught. The trek took two snowmobiles, pulling sleds. When the fishing was slow the kids would climb the steep hills and slide to the bottom.

Virginia said, "Duane and I went to a lot of remote speckled trout lakes and caught a lot of nice fish. We called the lakes by different names, like Secret Lake 1, or Secret Lake 2, or 10, so the kids couldn't broadcast where we were fishing. We went fishing on Pigeon Bay once in the summer, and Duane tied onto a big fish. It turned out to be a white fish. It was a hot day so he cleaned it right away and put it on ice. It most likely would have been a state record, ten and one-half pounds dressed.

"We were fishing in Lake Superior, and I tied into a big steel-head, which most likely would have been a record too. Steelheads are a lot of fun to catch, but not too great to eat. I caught a ten-pound Chinook salmon on Lake Superior, and that was really fun."

Another lake the Johnsons liked to fish was Lost Lake. Virginia caught a five pound, two ounce splake through the ice and won $100.00 in a fishing contest, buying an ice auger with the winnings. Now, in Virginia's words, "The state goofed and didn't keep an access point on the lake, so now it is all private and we can't fish there anymore."

I'd like to explain now that a "splake" is a hybrid of two differ-ent fish species: a male brook trout and a female lake trout.

In the fall, the Johnsons would go to Arrow Lake in Canada, fishing for white fish and lake trout, casting from the shore at dif-ferent points. At times, it would snow and turn very cold, but the five-pound fish were fun to catch. One October, Duane and a friend made the trip to Arrow Lake, and got caught in a blizzard, dump-ing at least a foot of snow. Most of the roads were closed, forcing them to circumnavigate, but the catch was a good one, and well worth the trip.

Carlson's Creek runs through the Johnson property, with a falls up the creek, where the steelhead try jumping up. They never make it, but it's a good show to watch.

Long ago, when Duane was involved in taking people out for lake fishing, a party hooked onto a large fish, with the man unable to even turn the reel against the force of the fish. That's incredible because the reel had a three-to-one-gear ratio. Duane had to help by pulling the line by hand between the first eye and the reel; with the fisherman reeling in the slack. It took about twenty minutes to finally get the fish landed, and had two hook barbs in the dorsal fin from previous catches. The fish weighed in at about twenty-two pounds, but in those days, the usual weight went around twenty pounds. Those were the days before the deadly lamprey killed off the larger game fish.

Another unusual thrill for Duane came when he was fishing the river, and, as he pulled his hook out of the water, a steelhead followed the hook over a rock and snapped onto it. They would tell the kids that if they spotted a fish, all they had to do was run and the fish will come flying out.

When it's not time to fish, it's certainly time to hunt. The Johnsons love the exhilaration that a hunting trip provides. The hunt is as important as the game taken because of it. From knowing where the party is spread out to becoming one with the environment that surrounds them, the hunters are looking for food and will condemn the taking of animal life that is not fair and sporting. The purpose of taking game is to provide for the family. Being together with the family is the magnum opus of life.

In keeping with the morals of a good hunt, Virginia recalls one particular trip with Duane. "Duane and I were hunting deer. I sat on a stump while he went out on a drive. Two deer came running through, so I shot the first one and it dropped right down. The other one circled around and I shot it, but I didn't know for sure if he dropped. When Duane got back we figured we needed to look for the second one first and found him dead. We pulled it out, and went for the first one. The deer hadn't moved in that time, but when we got up to it, he jumped up and ran. We tracked him for two hours before we caught up to him, when I had to shoot him again. The tracking was more difficult because there was no snow, but we had to do it."

Just this year, Duane went to one of the three gardens they keep, to find everything trampled down and the corn eaten. Thinking the deer had gotten in, he sprayed a repellent, which seemed to keep the deer out. However, the repellent had a fish odor, and attracted a different animal. A truck driver passing by saw a bear sitting in the garden, eating like a king. Three hours later, he returned and saw the bear still sitting in place. Being bear season, there were bear bait stations on two sides of the garden, but the bear was more attracted to the vegetables that smelled like fish.

Chapter 17

Planting Seeds
The Beginning of a Town

Like any other spot on any map, a town is created because people settle there and create industry. Fields are plowed, houses are built, and commerce follows. Family roots are planted and that particular spot on God's earth becomes home. Populations flourish because in order to have enough hands to farm the fields, children are born with the expectations of their helping. Following out of necessity are schools, stores, churches, and more people to operate them. All of this happens because people are looking for a decent place to survive.

When the railroad reached Duluth, an avenue was created to open trade all along the North Shore. The steamships carried building supplies to the settlers and brought fish and timber back in return. In 1871, Henry Mayhew and Sam Howenstine arrived at the place where Grand Marais sits, to found a village and start a commercial fishing operation. All went well until the panic of 1873 ended their effort. The effect was widespread with the population of Duluth dwindling to 1300 people.

However, there were people who still moved forward, and as usual, the economy started thriving again. In 1888, Ole Brunes and

Nels Ludwig Eliasen, two Norwegian carpenters from Duluth, built a log cabin on Brunes's homestead at Hovland. The single cabin housed the two families until the Eliasen home was finished on the adjoining homestead.

The year 1889 marks when the first post office was created, making Hovland the oldest organized township in Cook County. The town's original name was Chicago, but the name was rejected by locals because it sounded too much like a corruption of the Ojibwe word *shikag/jikag*, which translates into "skunk." The name Hovland was chosen by Anna Brunes, after her grandfather's home in Norway.

History can only be passed on to the future by talking about it, recording it. Tapping into the minds of those who lived through times past, drawing out recollections and events to flesh out bones of recorded history ensures that our heritage is remembered.

In digging out information to make this story as complete as possible, I pestered anyone who would pay attention to me. As much of a nuisance as I was, there was never an adverse gesture from anyone. One day I walked into Marcia Lacey's yard to ask if we could take pictures of the old Ellingson Hotel, which sat on her property. She approached me, a total stranger, with a concerned look, asking, "Yes, may I help you?"

I told her I was putting together a book on the history of the area and the ancestors of Duane and Virginia Johnson.

The mention of the Johnson name was all it took to tell Marcia I was someone she could trust. A moment later we were in her home poring through a massive collection of newspaper clippings, photographs, and hundreds of artifacts. She escorted my wife and myself around and through the old hotel while we took pictures. We were able to witness the rooms as the first settlers saw them.

Unfortunately, due to the deterioration of time and the beatings from Lake Superior, the building likely will have to be razed soon. They have plans on saving as much as possible to use elsewhere, but the old building itself will be gone.

Marcia showed us the rest of their lake-shore place. They have one cabin available for rent.

Marcia loaned us a booklet put together to commemorate the sixtieth wedding anniversary of Mr. and Mrs. August Brunes, in 1970.

The following is an excerpt from what he titled, "My Memories," written as closely following August's own words as possible.

The carpenter trade that Ole Brunes followed at Duluth, paid so poorly that he and Ludwig Eliasen, who followed the same trade, decided to quit that trade and fish for the market instead. They built themselves a twenty-six-foot sailboat and left their families at Duluth while they sailed up along the North Shore of Lake Superior, 130 miles from Duluth. There they decided to stay and take a homestead. The place was called Chicago Bay. There was not a living soul for miles. It was twenty miles to Grand Marais and seventeen miles to Grand Portage. They hewed out of the brush and timber, creating a small clearing where they built their first log house, a one-room building sixteen by eighteen feet with two small windows and a door made of hewn logs, a floor of hewn logs, and a roof made of poles overlaid with bark. This first house cost them less than $10.00. The windows were all they bought.

When the house was finished, Mr. Eliasen brought his family first, then later Ole Brunes brought his family, and they all lived together in that small log house for several months until Eliasen got his house built on his homestead, a two-room log house. "We stayed on in our one-room house until father got his two-room log house built. I'll never forget how happy we were to move into that house. Father made cupboards with drawers in the kitchen. Father and Mother slept in the front room, and us kids slept in the attic. We had to climb a ladder to get up there through a two-foot square cubby hole.

The A. Booth & Co. Fisheries at Duluth had a tramp steamer, the *Dixon*, that made regular trips up the North Shore, bringing supplies to the fishermen and buying their fish. All communication had to come by the way of the steamer until a post office was established at

Hovland. My mother named it Hovland, so then Chicago Bay passed out of the picture. Father was the first postmaster and continued until we left Hovland in 1903."

Author's note: The corruption of the term "Chicago" has been illustrated. The correct name of the town Norway may very well have been spelled "Hoveland," but the spelling "Hovland" has been established for the town.

"I was between six and seven years old when we came to Hoveland [sic], and, at the age of ten years, Louis Eliasen said to Father he was going to get along with his oldest son, Hjalmar, as his fishing partner (he was eleven) so that left no other choice for my father but to take me as his partner—a barefoot boy of ten years. There was a big write up in the *Duluth Evening Herald* about me being the youngest fisherman on Lake Superior. I was too young to row the heavy boat along the set lines, so I had to do all the lifting of the lines and change all the herring baits for new ones. I'll never forget that first summer, how I'd get sea sick but could not stop my work for that—no time to vomit. All in a day's work.

"One day we had just finished our set lines when a strong west wind blew up. We were ready to set sail for shore. I was holding the tiller while Father hoisted the sails. It was foggy so we could not see the shore. I was sure our boat was heading the wrong way, so I turned the rudder, and the boom of the main sail came and struck Father, almost knocking him overboard. He gave me a lecture on handling a sailboat that I never forgot. Neither of us could swim, so that was a near tragedy. In ice water seven or eight miles from shore, we could have both perished.

"There were many hard lessons to learn that first spring and summer, and it seems that I learned them all the hard way. I think it was about the same time that Mother was in the family way and a month or so before Sophia was born. Father said for me to go with him in the sailboat to Grand Marais to get the mid-wife. So, of course, we had to dress up to go to town. I had knee pants with long stockings (home knit). The weather was cold that spring, so I could not go barefoot. I had no shoes to put on and Father made me wear Mother's peaked high top button shoes. When we got to the general store in Grand Marais, I was so embarrassed it seemed that everyone was looking at me, but I lived through it. We brought Mrs. Anaquette, an Indian woman, home to stay with us in that one-room log house until Sophie was born and Mother could get along. When it came time to pay the Indian woman she bargained up to $5.00.

"One day my siblings and I saw a large animal up in a tree. We ran and told Father and Eliasen. They came with their muskets to shoot a big bear (so we thought). Mr. Eliasen shot it, but what came tumbling down was a big porcupine—what a letdown! Big game was scarce in those days. The deer and moose came in as the country settled. There were some stray caribou. Otherwise, for fresh meat we snared rabbits, which were plentiful, and also partridges. Of course, we ate quite a lot of fish in those days. Fish was cheap. Choice trout three cents a pound. Large trout head cut off brought us two cents a pound. Herring we had to clean, wash good and salt down in 100-pound kegs for $1.50 keg. Kegs and salt were furnished by the fish company. It was not long until other fishermen moved to Chicago Bay.

"I remember our first schoolhouse when I was about twelve years old. It was a small one-room log house with low eves, so it was easy for us to climb up on the almost-flat roof. Our teacher was Mr. Fowler, who was about fifty years old. The kids did not like him, and we got into trouble with him."

Mr. Brunes goes on with some interesting comments on how life was at the time:

"Our next teacher was Mrs. Lester, and our school was a larger log house with a bedroom where she stayed. She was a pretty good teacher. I could not go to school until after the steamer quit for the winter, which was about December first, so I had five months schooling each year for three or four years."

August Brunes goes into details of their life in Hovland, such as going to Duluth to buy a cow. "We took her on the steamer as far as Grand Marais and from there to Havland (twenty miles). It was my job to follow with the "persuader" (a switch). At one point we had to cross water by the lake side of the Brule River. Father waded in, and I persuaded the cow to do likewise. The water came up to father's chest. The cow swam and I held onto her tail as there was quite a current, and it was hard for me to keep my feet on the bottom. This was the first cow in Hovland, so it was quite a celebration. Mother took over care of the cow as she was the only one who knew how to milk."

Of significant interest are details of the commerce brought by the steamship *America*, since it played such an important role in the development of Hovland. It became August's job to row his skiff out to the ship to haul supplies and passengers, mostly lumberjacks, to shore.

August writes, "The steamer always got to Hovland about one o'clock in the morning. The captain would toot the horn to wake me up, and sometimes if I was a little slow in dressing, he would turn the floodlights on our house. I would have to row out quite a long ways from shore as the captain was afraid to bring the steamer very close. In the fall when the lumber camp started up, there was a lot of freight to haul ashore, bailed hay, sacks of feed, logging sleds.

"The steamer *America* stopped about December first and the steamer *Moor*, which was smaller, took over the hauling until the ice froze too thick to navigate. On Christmas Eve the Moor tooted for me to come out. There was a northwest storm brewing — colder weather. They had a load of supplies for a lumber camp five miles east of Hovland. They pulled my skiff aboard, and when we got to the camp we used their eighteen-foot skiff and the *Moor*'s skiff to deliver the freight. This was done for about two hours until the storm got too rough. I was the last load in, and the *Moor* was drifting out where it was really rough. They threw the line to me, pulled my boat up in the first deck, closed the heavy gangway doors and started for Grand

Marais. The captain said he could not stop at Hovland as it was getting too rough.

"It took us many hours to make those twenty-five miles. The windows in the lounge were broken by flying ice, so we nailed canvas over them. About an hour before we got to Grand Marais, the captain came in from the pilot house to warm up. When he went out, he could not shut the heavy door. The door flapped back and forth until we got hold of the handle. One hinge was broken, so the deck hands tied a rope to the door handle. Then the other hinge broke and the wind flapped the door around like a piece of paper until we finally got the door inside. We nailed it in place with boards.

"As we listened to the storm outside, the steamer gave a lurch, the keel scraped bottom, and the next thing we knew there was a crash. Our steamer was pushed over against another steamer."

August describes how the wind and ice had broken open the gangway doors and his skiff was blown away. This is an excellent first hand account of the fury that can rage on Lake Superior. At home, his family searched the shoreline for him and thought he had perished in the storm. He arrived home from Grand Marais the next day.

The Dock

THE STEAMSHIPS PLAYED A HUGE ROLE in the development of Hovland, but the dock in Chicago Bay was equally important. Unloading passengers and cargo from the ships required significant efforts. Rowing skiffs out to the ships in all climates was not an effective process, or particularly safe. The wooden dock was erected in 1905 and the concrete pier built over it in 1912. The following is taken from a brochure by the Hovland Dock Committee in their effort to find funding for a restoration project:

"The dock remained valued and pivotal to Hovland until the 1950s, when sport fishing filled the harbor with trolling boats and small

The Hovland dock, September 3, 1972.

The Hovland dock as it stands today.

Top and above. At the shore of the Hovland dock today.

113

The graves of Charles and Alice Bray in the Hovland cemetery.

skiffs. With the invasion of the lamprey eel, the Hovland economy began to fail in the 1960s, and fishing was no longer a way of life for most.

"In the early 1970s the new layer of concrete was added to the surface of the dock, and the warehouse torn down.

"In the fall of 1996 a devastating lake storm hit the entire North Shore. For nearly three days, the dock was mercilessly pounded, the end lifted off its cribbing and slammed down again, breaking loose and shifting the last fifty feet of the 200-foot structure. This is how it stands today."

Hovland

THE TOWN OF HOVLAND ONCE CAME very close to extinction. Typical for many small towns in the early years of the Depression, large numbers of citizens could not pay their taxes. More and more real estate was removed from the assessment rolls, year after year. Much land was taken over by the federal and state governments, forcing county tax levy rates up in an effort to keep government functioning. Inflated tax bills made them all but unpayable for many citizens, leading to more delinquency. This cycle was certain to lead to bankruptcy and collapse of local government, a situation all too familiar to people in 2008 and 2009.

A Booth Line steamer, probably the *Moore* at the Hovland dock.

In January 1928, the Hovland town clerk, N.J. Bray, received a letter from the county auditor stating that a "communication with twelve signers" had been delivered to the county commissioners, "asking the county coard to dissolve the town of Hovland." Auditor

A tug putting together a raft of logs at Hovland.

T.F. Thomas notified the clerk that a hearing on the matter would be held at the court fouse, February 14, 1928.

The leaders in town at the time were Supervisors, Frank Kuger, Andrew Myhr, Oscar Sundquist, and clerk N.J. Bray. In desperate preparation, on January 21st, signatures were put to a letter to county officials voicing their resistance to the whole idea of dissolution. An exact copy of the wording of that letter is on display in the Hovland Town Hall.

The letter to the county officials was effective, causing them to, "Indefinitely postpone the sensitive matter."

However, the supervisors had reason to believe that the dissolution idea remained a threat. In an effort to prove the financial stability of the town, they published figures on March 6, 1928, which seemed to prove their case. Outstanding dock bonds: $7,000. McFarland Lake Road bonds: $15,000. The total tax valuation of the town (according to figures from the county auditor at the end of 1927): $201,196.

The Moose Valley school, N.J. Bray teacher.

Arthur Johnson fishing at the Reservation River in the spring of 1916. A forest fire had gone through the area earlier that year.

On March 14, 1928, the entire Hovland town board, including the clerk, went to Duluth to engage legal counsel, "to protect and defend the rights of the town." They retained the services of "Baldwin, Baldwin, Holmes, and Mayall to institute a suit against the county board to prevent the dissolution.

The county board's case was stated forcefully in a two-column, "Open Letter to taxpayers of Hovland Town," two months after it was written, on May 17, 1928, in the *News Herald*. To sum up the board's reasoning, they said that after the timber companies strip the land of trees, they will abandon the area, leaving the taxpayers unable to support their government.

On March 24, 1928, a petition was sent to Judge C.R. Magney, asking for his support. On a motion by the lawyer, D.S. Holmes, Judge Magney dismissed the case. After notices from county board chairman, Hans O. Engelsen, and assistant Minnesota attorney general, W.H. Gurnee, the Hovland town board had won their fight.

Martin Jacobsen at the switchboard at Hovland.

The Pigeon River Lumber Company camp, McFarland Lake.

Hovland school, circa 1905.

Art Eliasen with a flat tire.

Making hay at Hovland, circa 1915.

Adolph S. Carlson, one of the founders of Hovland, 1900.

Taken directly from the account on display in the Hovland Town Hall, "The proud, stubborn farmers and fishermen of Hovland were the inheritors of the oldest town in Cook County. Since its first town meeting, January 22, 1894, it had continued the outspoken individualistic traditions first defended by men like, Nels Ludwig Eliasen, his brothers Emil and John, by Ole Brunes, Adolph Carlson, Fred Jackson, Johan Jacobsen, and John McFarland. For more than a generation after the turn of the century, extensive

Martin Jacobsen's store at Chicago Bay, Hovland, in 1935.

logging operations in the area kept Hovland the colorful boom-town on the North Shore.

The town had become relatively safe from being dissolved, but the controversy kept coming up for many years.

The Bank Robbers

Ray Bowman and Billy Kirkpatrick teamed up as bank robbers, and were wanted for escapades all over the Midwest and the West Coast. One heist in the state of Washington netted them over four-million dollars.

Billy Kirkpatrick and his girl friend, Myra Penney, were staking out a bank in Duluth in 1988. Both fell in love with the North Shore, deciding to settle down there. In 1994 they built a cedar log home on the shores of Lake Superior, in the town of Hovland, hiring builder Michael Senty to do the construction. Senty thought they were nice enough people but found it odd that Penney always paid him in cash. Fifty and hundred dollar bills to be precise, all rolled up and bound with rubber bands and tucked into a brown paper lunch bag were given to Senty as payment.

Kirkpatrick and Penney became friends with neighbors, Randy and Monica Schnobrich, often trading baby sitting with each other.

Kathi Johnson tells of the amazing salsa recipe she got from Monica, who got it from Penney. To this day, it is one of the favorite flavors at the Johnson home.

Things took a turn for worse for Kirkpatrick and Penney when she took to relentlessly hounding Senty about finishing touches. Finding her behavior irritating, and the amount of cash passing from her suspicious, an anonymous call to the IRS started the unhinging of the bank robbers.

Kirkpatrick's partner, Ray Bowman, was eventually caught as well, with both serving prison sentences.

Roots

WHEN THE SUNDQUISTS, the Johnsons, the Bergsvens, and the Schuppels came to Minnesota they weren't looking for anything more than a place to set their roots. America offered countless pioneers escape from something or the satisfaction of a new life. People came for their own reasons and stayed for their own reasons. After landing at Chicago Bay, these pioneers had no choice but to move inland.

There were no roads, the teams were stopped by dense forests, they faced pests and dangers, but they stayed. They moved inland to claim one of the most sought after commodities, their very own piece of earth. On the very first day, standing before the trees towering over them, feet planted firmly on the earth they sought, they didn't say, "Let's go home." The only option open to them was to settle in and build a life.

At no time was life easy, and nothing was handed to them. In the case of Ida Sundquist Johnson, stranded in the wilderness with small

Lake Superior from Pat's Cove.

children to raise, she was never given the choice to quit. With pure determination, she did what all the others did, met tomorrow with the need to survive and got through it.

When transportation was nonexistent, Werner Sundquist, Andrew Westerlund, and Jacob Soderlund would walk to earn a days pay, and then walk home at the end of the day. Mary Sundquist, widowed with young Oscar working on a road gang at age nine, was nothing but determination to survive. August Johnson, who walked from Hovland to Duluth, was just doing what needed to be done.

Nobody was considered a hero.

If anyone wonders what values this country was founded on, they need look no further than the relentless pioneers who turned a wilderness into a home. This is what I saw in the two people who

123

floated across a dance floor in a small northern Minnesota town. This is what I saw in the children they raised who have the same values their ancestors had. Whatever there is that needs to be done, it happens because that is the way of life that loving and devoted parents seasoned them with.

The salt of the earth.

Pat's Cove. Judge Edward F. Waite's log cabin, circa 1920.

Judge Waite entertaining guests at Pat's Cove cabin.

Hovland Post Office, John Eliasen, postmaster until 1914.

Dog Sled Trail near Pat's Cove, Hovland.

Workers and the owners of the Ellingsen Hotel in Hovland on the hotel lawn for a picture. Left to right: Cook Conrad Moen, Lena Ellingsen (Arnquist), John Jacobsen, unknown, Mrs. Louise Nellie Ellingsen, Hilmer Nelson, and "Dog." Circa 1940. (Photo courtesy Cook County Historical Society)

A 1950s photo of the Hovland dock, showing a long-gone level of activity for commercial fishing and pleasure boating. (Photo courtesy the Cook County Historical Society)

School days at the Chicago Bay School.

School days at the Moose Valley School in 1911, taught by N.J. Bray (second from right).

Contributors

Without the sincere devotion of these people who want to preserve the history of their town and the families that built it, stories like this one would never be written. They have entrusted me with their personal family artifacts and memories. I thank them and give all due respect and credit for their dedication.

~

Dusty Nelms. Her years of unflagging work of digging into the history and genealogy of her family are the backbone of *Salt of the Earth*. It all stemmed from her intense love for her family.

Duane and Virginia Johnson. If I could ever be compared to anyone, I could only hope it would be to these two awesome people. Virginia's incredible memory and Duane's staunch conviction and belief in good work are the backbone of his family and this little town. Virginia wrote countless pages of hand written notes on yellow legal sheets to chronicle hundreds of details pulled from her memory.

Marcia Lacey. At the mere suggestion that I was interested in doing this book, Marcia was more than eager to share her home and treasures with us. She is of the same stalwart character that the Johnson family is made of. For a pleasurable water front vacation, I would recommend checking out her website. Chicago Bay Hideaway, Hovland, MN www.chicagobayhideaway.com

Millie Mainella. Whose recollection of her past and fond memories of the life she has so joyously shared with us.

Barb Hirsch. For the wonderful essay she composed called, "Meet A Parishioner," which detailed so many memories of Aunt Millie.

Amy Neilsen. Her efforts, along with the other members of the Hovland Dock Restoration Project, are struggling to save the landmark that greeted the settlers. Even in its decayed state, it is worth the effort to take a look at it. If you want to get involved in the project, contact: "Hovland Dock Restoration, PO Box 582, Hovland, MN 55606."

Alice Moren. Who graciously allowed the use of the booklet presented at her father Art Sundquist's eighty-fifth birthday.

Lisa Messenbring: Owner of the Chicago Bay Marketplace, 4971 East Hwy 61, Hovland, MN 55606. The home made bread, exotic beer, and wonderful food, are worthy of a stop on your way to anywhere. You can browse through the history of Hovland gazing at the photo's covering the walls. There is also the likelihood that an old-timer will be sitting nearby to elucidate on the characters in each photo.

Rusty and Kathi Johnson: It was my admiration for the strong character of Rusty and Kathi that prompted me to even think about doing this. I learned of the "salsa and the bank robber" connection from Kathi. She also was more than generous in loaning documents and photos.

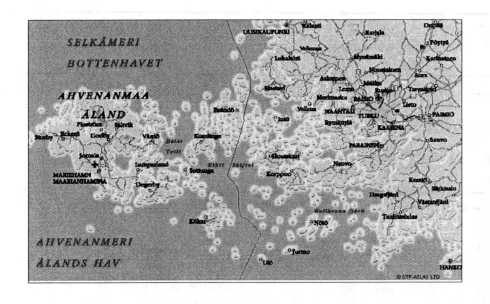

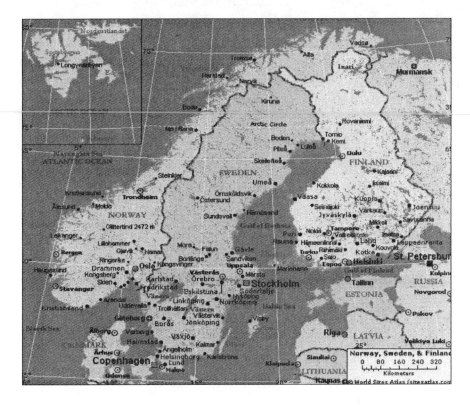

Pastor Kristin Garey. Trinity Evangelical Lutheran Church in America, Hovland, Minnesota. Her faith, good humor, and devotion to the Trinity Lutheran Church and its parishioners, are deeply appreciated. The address is: 4957 East Hwy 61, Hovland, MN 55606. trinity@boreal.org to order your copy of the one-hundred-year anniversary book.

If there is an interest in the history of the church, I recommend contacting the church for a copy of the excellent book commemorating the event.

> Trinity Lutheran Church
> PO Box 188
> Hovland, MN 55606
> Email: trinity@boreal.org
> www.trinitylutheranofhovland.org

Bob and Jeanine Swearingen. Bob is one of my closest friends, and I enjoy sitting with him sharing a cup of coffee, discussing history from any place that our memories will take us. I love Bob and Jeanine very much, and take a short liberty here to let them both know that in spite of the roller coaster ride of life, the car is still securely attached to the track. I still have your book on Lake Superior, Bob. My hanging on to it longer than I should is just another reason to get together.